Lambert M. Surhone, Mariam T. Tennoe,
Susan F. Henssonow (Ed.)

Lightweight Software Test Automation

Lambert M. Surhone, Mariam T. Tennoe,
Susan F. Henssonow (Ed.)

Lightweight Software Test Automation

Computer Programs, Test Automation, IMacros

Betascript Publishing

Imprint

All parts of this book are extracted from Wikipedia, the free encyclopedia (www.wikipedia.org).

You can get detailed informations about the authors of this collection of articles at the end of this book. The editors (Ed.) of this book are no authors. They have not modified or extended the original texts.

Pictures published in this book can be under different licences than the GNU Free Documentation License. You can get detailed informations about the authors and licences of pictures at the end of this book.

The content of this book was generated collaboratively by volunteers. Please be advised that nothing found here has necessarily been reviewed by people with the expertise required to provide you with complete, accurate or reliable information. Some information in this book maybe misleading or wrong. The Publisher does not guarantee the validity of the information found here. If you need specific advice (f.e. in fields of medical, legal, financial, or risk management questions) please contact a professional who is licensed or knowledgeable in that area.

Cover image: www.ingimage.com
Concerning the licence of the cover image please contact ingimage.

Contact:
VDM Publishing House Ltd.,17 Rue Meldrum, Beau Bassin,1713-01 Mauritius
Email: info@vdm-publishing-house.com
Website: www.vdm-publishing-house.com

Published in 2010
Printed in: U.S.A., U.K., Germany. This book was not produced in Mauritius.

ISBN: 978-613-4-54130-5

Contents

Articles

References

Article Licenses

Lightweight software test automation

Lightweight software test automation is the process of creating and using relatively short and simple computer programs, called lightweight test harnesses, designed to test a software system. Lightweight test automation harnesses are not tied to a particular programming language but are most often implemented with the Java, Perl, Visual Basic .NET, and C# programming languages. Lightweight test automation harnesses are generally four pages of source code or less, and are generally written in four hours or less. Lightweight test automation is often associated with Agile software development methodology.

The three major alternatives to the use of lightweight software test automation are commercial test automation frameworks, Open Source test automation frameworks, and heavyweight test automation. The primary disadvantage of lightweight test automation is manageability. Because lightweight automation is relatively quick and easy to implement, a test effort can be overwhelmed with harness programs, test case data files, test result files, and so on. However, lightweight test automation has significant advantages. Compared with commercial frameworks, lightweight automation is less expensive in initial cost and is more flexible. Compared with Open Source frameworks, lightweight automation is more stable because there are fewer updates and external dependencies. Compared with heavyweight test automation, lightweight automation is quicker to implement and modify. Lightweight test automation is generally used to complement, not replace these alternative approaches.

Lightweight test automation is most useful for regression testing, where the intention is to verify that new source code added to the system under test has not created any new software failures. Lightweight test automation may be used for other areas of software testing such as performance testing, stress testing, load testing, security testing, code coverage analysis, mutation testing, and so on. The most widely published proponent of the use of lightweight software test automation is Dr. James D. McCaffrey.

References

- Definition and characteristics of lightweight software test automation in: McCaffrey, James D., ".NET Test Automation Recipes", Apress Publishing, 2006. ISBN: 1590596633.
- Discussion of lightweight test automation versus manual testing in: Patton, Ron, "Software Testing, 2nd ed.", Sams Publishing, 2006. ISBN: 0672327988.
- An example of lightweight software test automation for .NET applications: "Lightweight UI Test Automation with .NET", MSDN Magazine, January 2005 (Vol. 20, No. 1). See http://msdn2.microsoft.com/en-us/magazine/cc163864.aspx.
- A demonstration of lightweight software test automation applied to stress testing: "Stress Testing", MSDN Magazine, May 2006 (Vol. 21, No. 6). See http://msdn2.microsoft.com/en-us/magazine/cc163613.aspx.
- A discussion of lightweight software test automation for performance testing: "Web App Diagnostics: Lightweight Automated Performance Analysis", asp.netPRO Magazine, August 2005 (Vol. 4, No. 8).
- An example of lightweight software test automation for Web applications: "Lightweight UI Test Automation for ASP.NET Web Applications", MSDN Magazine, April 2005 (Vol. 20, No. 4). See http://msdn2.microsoft.com/en-us/magazine/cc163814.aspx.
- A technique for mutation testing using lightweight software test automation: "Mutant Power: Create a Simple Mutation Testing System with the .NET Framework", MSDN Magazine, April 2006 (Vol. 21, No. 5). See http://msdn2.microsoft.com/en-us/magazine/cc163619.aspx.
- An investigation of lightweight software test automation in a scripting environment: "Lightweight Testing with Windows PowerShell", MSDN Magazine, May 2007 (Vol. 22, No. 5). See http://msdn2.microsoft.com/en-us/magazine/cc163430.aspx.

See also

- Test automation
- Microsoft Visual Test
- iMacros
- Software Testing

Computer programs

A **computer program** (also a **software program**, or just a **program**) is a sequence of instructions written to perform a specified task for a computer.[1] A computer requires programs to function, typically executing the program's instructions in a central processor.[2] The program has an executable form that the computer can use directly to execute the instructions. The same program in its human-readable source code form, from which executable programs are derived (e.g., compiled), enables a programmer to study and develop its algorithms.

Computer source code is often written by computer programmers. Source code is written in a programming language that usually follows one of two main paradigms: imperative or declarative programming. Source code may be converted into an executable file (sometimes called an executable program or a binary) by a compiler and later executed by a central processing unit. Alternatively, computer programs may be executed with the aid of an interpreter, or may be embedded directly into hardware.

Computer programs may be categorized along functional lines: system software and application software. Two or more computer programs may run simultaneously on one computer, a process known as multitasking.

Programming

```
#include <stdio.h>
int main()
{
printf("Hello world!\n");
return 0;
}
```

Source code of a program written in the C programming language

Computer programming is the iterative process of writing or editing source code. Editing source code involves testing, analyzing, and refining, and sometimes coordinating with other programmers on a jointly developed program. A person who practices this skill is referred to as a computer programmer, software developer or coder. The sometimes lengthy process of computer programming is usually referred to as software development. The term software engineering is becoming popular as the process is seen as an engineering discipline.

Paradigms

Computer programs can be categorized by the programming language paradigm used to produce them. Two of the main paradigms are imperative and declarative.

Programs written using an imperative language specify an algorithm using declarations, expressions, and statements.[3] A declaration couples a variable name to a datatype. For example: var x: integer; . An expression yields a value. For example: 2 + 2 yields 4. Finally, a statement might assign an expression to a variable or use the value of a variable to alter the program's control flow. For example: x := 2 + 2; if x = 4 then do_something(); One criticism of imperative languages is the side effect of an assignment statement on a class of variables called non-local variables.[4]

Programs written using a declarative language specify the properties that have to be met by the output. They do not specify details expressed in terms of the control flow of the executing machine but of the mathematical relations between the declared objects and their properties. Two broad categories of declarative languages are functional languages and logical languages. The principle behind functional languages (like Haskell) is to not allow side effects, which makes it easier to reason about programs like mathematical functions.[4] The principle behind logical languages (like Prolog) is to define the problem to be solved — the goal — and leave the detailed solution to the Prolog system itself.[5] The goal is defined by providing a list of subgoals. Then each subgoal is defined by further providing a list of its subgoals, etc. If a path of subgoals fails to find a solution, then that subgoal is backtracked and another path is systematically attempted.

The form in which a program is created may be textual or visual. In a visual language program, elements are graphically manipulated rather than textually specified.

Compiling or interpreting

A *computer program* in the form of a human-readable, computer programming language is called source code. Source code may be converted into an executable image by a compiler or executed immediately with the aid of an interpreter.

Either compiled or interpreted programs might be executed in a batch process without human interaction, but interpreted programs allow a user to type commands in an interactive session. In this case the programs are the separate commands, whose execution occurs sequentially, and thus together. When a language is used to give commands to a software application (such as a shell) it is called a scripting language.

Compiled computer programs are commonly referred to as executables, binary images, or simply as binaries — a reference to the binary file format used to store the executable code. Compilers are used to translate source code from a programming language into either object code or machine code. Object code needs further processing to become machine code, and machine code is the central processing unit's native code, ready for execution.

Interpreted computer programs -in a batch or interactive session- are either decoded and then immediately executed or are decoded into some efficient intermediate representation for future execution. BASIC, Perl, and Python are examples of immediately executed computer programs. Alternatively, Java computer programs are compiled ahead of time and stored as a machine independent code called bytecode. Bytecode is then executed on request by an interpreter called a virtual machine.

The main disadvantage of interpreters is that computer programs run slower than when compiled. Interpreting code is slower than running the compiled version because the interpreter must decode each statement each time it is loaded and then perform the desired action. However, software development may be faster using an interpreter because testing is immediate when the compiling step is omitted. Another disadvantage of interpreters is that at least one must be present on the computer during computer program execution. By contrast, compiled computer programs need no compiler present during execution.

No properties of a programming language require it to be exclusively compiled or exclusively interpreted. The categorization usually reflects the most popular method of language execution. For example, BASIC is thought of as an interpreted language and C a compiled language, despite the existence of BASIC compilers and C interpreters. Some systems use just-in-time compilation (JIT) whereby sections of the source are compiled 'on the fly' and stored for subsequent executions.

Self-modifying programs

A computer program in execution is normally treated as being different from the data the program operates on. However, in some cases this distinction is blurred when a computer program modifies itself. The modified computer program is subsequently executed as part of the same program. Self-modifying code is possible for programs written in machine code, assembly language, Lisp, C, COBOL, PL/1, Prolog and JavaScript (the eval feature) among others.

Execution and storage

Typically, computer programs are stored in non-volatile memory until requested either directly or indirectly to be executed by the computer user. Upon such a request, the program is loaded into random access memory, by a computer program called an operating system, where it can be accessed directly by the central processor. The central processor then executes ("runs") the program, instruction by instruction, until termination. A program in execution is called a process.[6] Termination is either by normal self-termination or by error — software or hardware error.

Embedded programs

The microcontroller on the right of this USB flash drive is controlled with embedded firmware.

Some computer programs are embedded into hardware. A stored-program computer requires an initial computer program stored in its read-only memory to boot. The boot process is to identify and initialize all aspects of the system, from processor registers to device controllers to memory contents.[7] Following the initialization process, this initial computer program loads the operating system and sets the program counter to begin normal operations. Independent of the host computer, a hardware device might have embedded firmware to control its operation. Firmware is used when the computer program is rarely or never expected to change, or when the program must not be lost when the power is off.[8]

Manual programming

Computer programs historically were manually input to the central processor via switches. An instruction was represented by a configuration of on/off settings. After setting the configuration, an execute button was pressed. This process was then repeated. Computer programs also historically were manually input via paper tape or punched cards. After the medium was loaded, the starting address was set via switches and the execute button pressed.[9]

Switches for manual input on a Data General Nova 3

Automatic program generation

Generative programming is a style of computer programming that creates source code through generic classes, prototypes, templates, aspects, and code generators to improve programmer productivity. Source code is generated with programming tools such as a template processor or an integrated development environment. The simplest form of source code generator is a macro processor, such as the C preprocessor, which replaces patterns in source code according to relatively simple rules.

Software engines output source code or markup code that simultaneously become the input to another computer process. The analogy is that of one process driving another process, with the computer code being burned as fuel. Application servers are software engines that deliver applications to client computers. For example, a Wiki is an application server that lets users build dynamic content assembled from articles. Wikis generate HTML, CSS, Java, and JavaScript which are then interpreted by a web browser.

Simultaneous execution

Many operating systems support multitasking which enables many computer programs to appear to run simultaneously on one computer. Operating systems may run multiple programs through process scheduling — a software mechanism to switch the CPU among processes often so users can interact with each program while it runs.[10] Within hardware, modern day multiprocessor computers or computers with multicore processors may run multiple programs.[11]

One computer program can calculate simultaneously more than one operation using threads or separate processes. Multithreading processors are optimized to execute multiple threads efficiently.

Functional categories

Computer programs may be categorized along functional lines. The main functional categories are system software and application software. System software includes the operating system which couples computer hardware with application software.[12] The purpose of the operating system is to provide an environment in which application software executes in a convenient and efficient manner.[12] In addition to the operating system, system software includes utility programs that help manage and tune the computer. If a computer program is not system software then it is application software. Application software includes middleware, which couples the system software with the user interface. Application software also includes utility programs that help users solve application problems, like the need for sorting.

Sometimes development environments for software development are seen as a functional category on its own, especially in the context of human-computer interaction and programming language design. Development environments gather system software (such as compilers and system's batch processing scripting languages) and application software (such as IDEs) for the specific purpose of helping programmers create new programs.

See also

- Algorithm for the relationship between computer programs and algorithms
- Computer software for more information on computer programs
- Data structure

References

[1] Stair, Ralph M., et al. (2003). *Principles of Information Systems, Sixth Edition*. Thomson Learning, Inc.. pp. 132. ISBN 0-619-06489-7.
[2] Silberschatz, Abraham (1994). *Operating System Concepts, Fourth Edition*. Addison-Wesley. pp. 58. ISBN 0-201-50480-4.
[3] Wilson, Leslie B. (1993). *Comparative Programming Languages, Second Edition*. Addison-Wesley. pp. 75. ISBN 0-201-56885-3.
[4] Wilson, Leslie B. (1993). *Comparative Programming Languages, Second Edition*. Addison-Wesley. pp. 213. ISBN 0-201-56885-3.
[5] Wilson, Leslie B. (1993). *Comparative Programming Languages, Second Edition*. Addison-Wesley. pp. 244. ISBN 0-201-56885-3.
[6] Silberschatz, Abraham (1994). *Operating System Concepts, Fourth Edition*. Addison-Wesley. pp. 97. ISBN 0-201-50480-4.
[7] Silberschatz, Abraham (1994). *Operating System Concepts, Fourth Edition*. Addison-Wesley. pp. 30. ISBN 0-201-50480-4.
[8] Tanenbaum, Andrew S. (1990). *Structured Computer Organization, Third Edition*. Prentice Hall. pp. 11. ISBN 0-13-854662-2.
[9] Silberschatz, Abraham (1994). *Operating System Concepts, Fourth Edition*. Addison-Wesley. pp. 6. ISBN 0-201-50480-4.
[10] Silberschatz, Abraham (1994). *Operating System Concepts, Fourth Edition*. Addison-Wesley. pp. 100. ISBN 0-201-50480-4.
[11] Akhter, Shameem (2006). *Multi-Core Programming*. Richard Bowles (Intel Press). pp. 11–13. ISBN 0-9764832-4-6.
[12] Silberschatz, Abraham (1994). *Operating System Concepts, Fourth Edition*. Addison-Wesley. pp. 1. ISBN 0-201-50480-4.

Further reading

- Knuth, Donald E. (1997). *The Art of Computer Programming, Volume 1, 3rd Edition*. Boston: Addison-Wesley. ISBN 0-201-89683-4.
- Knuth, Donald E. (1997). *The Art of Computer Programming, Volume 2, 3rd Edition*. Boston: Addison-Wesley. ISBN 0-201-89684-2.
- Knuth, Donald E. (1997). *The Art of Computer Programming, Volume 3, 3rd Edition*. Boston: Addison-Wesley. ISBN 0-201-89685-0.

External links

- Definition of "Program" (http://www.webopedia.com/TERM/P/program.html) at Webopedia
- Definition of "Software" (http://wombat.doc.ic.ac.uk/foldoc/foldoc.cgi?query=software) at FOLDOC
- Definition of "Computer Program" (http://dictionary.reference.com/browse/computer program) at dictionary.com

Test automation

Compare with Manual testing.

Test automation is the use of software to control the execution of tests, the comparison of actual outcomes to predicted outcomes, the setting up of test preconditions, and other test control and test reporting functions[1] . Commonly, test automation involves automating a manual process already in place that uses a formalized testing process.

Overview

Although manual tests may find many defects in a software application, it is a laborious and time consuming process. In addition, it may not be effective in finding certain classes of defects. Test automation is a process of writing a computer program to do testing that would otherwise need to be done manually. Once tests have been automated, they can be run quickly. This is often the most cost effective method for software products that have a long maintenance life, because even minor patches over the lifetime of the application can cause features to break which were working at an earlier point in time.

There are two general approaches to test automation:

- **Code-driven testing**. The public (usually) interfaces to classes, modules, or libraries are tested with a variety of input arguments to validate that the results that are returned are correct.
- Graphical user interface testing. A testing framework generates user interface events such as keystrokes and mouse clicks, and observes the changes that result in the user interface, to validate that the observable behavior of the program is correct.

Test automation tools can be expensive, and it is usually employed in combination with manual testing. It can be made cost-effective in the longer term, especially when used repeatedly in regression testing.

One way to generate test cases automatically is model-based testing through use of a model of the system for test case generation but research continues into a variety of alternative methodologies for doing so.

What to automate, when to automate, or even whether one really needs automation are crucial decisions which the testing (or development) team must make. Selecting the correct features of the product for automation largely determines the success of the automation. Automating unstable features or features that are undergoing changes should be avoided.[2]

Code-driven testing

A growing trend in software development is the use of testing frameworks such as the xUnit frameworks (for example, JUnit and NUnit) that allow the execution of unit tests to determine whether various sections of the code are acting as expected under various circumstances. Test cases describe tests that need to be run on the program to verify that the program runs as expected.

Code driven test automation is a key feature of Agile software development, where it is known as Test-driven development (TDD). Unit tests are written to define the functionality *before* the code is written. Only when all tests pass is the code considered complete. Proponents argue that it produces software that is both more reliable and less costly than code that is tested by manual exploration. It is considered more reliable because the code coverage is better, and because it is run constantly during development rather than once at the end of a waterfall development cycle. The developer discovers defects immediately upon making a change, when it is least expensive to fix. Finally, code refactoring is safer; transforming the code into a simpler form with less code duplication, but equivalent behavior, is much less likely to introduce new defects.

Graphical User Interface (GUI) testing

Many test automation tools provide record and playback features that allow users to interactively record user actions and replay them back any number of times, comparing actual results to those expected. The advantage of this approach is that it requires little or no software development. This approach can be applied to any application that has a graphical user interface. However, reliance on these features poses major reliability and maintainability problems. Relabelling a button or moving it to another part of the window may require the test to be re-recorded. Record and playback also often adds irrelevant activities or incorrectly records some activities.

A variation on this type of tool is for testing of web sites. Here, the "interface" is the web page. This type of tool also requires little or no software development. However, such a framework utilizes entirely different techniques because it is reading html instead of observing window events.

Another variation is scriptless test automation that does not use record and playback, but instead builds a model of the application under test and then enables the tester to create test cases by simply editing in test parameters and conditions. This requires no scripting skills, but has all the power and flexibility of a scripted approach. Test-case maintenance is easy, as there is no code to maintain and as the application under test changes the software objects can simply be re-learned or added. It can be applied to any GUI-based software application.

What to test

Testing tools can help automate tasks such as product installation, test data creation, GUI interaction, problem detection (consider parsing or polling agents equipped with oracles), defect logging, etc., without necessarily automating tests in an end-to-end fashion.

One must keep satisfying popular requirements when thinking of test automation:

- Platform and OS independence
- Data driven capability (Input Data, Output Data, Meta Data)
- Customizable Reporting (DB Access, crystal reports)
- Easy debugging and logging
- Version control friendly – minimal binary files
- Extensible & Customizable (Open APIs to be able to integrate with other tools)
- Common Driver (For example, in the Java development ecosystem, that means Ant or Maven and the popular IDEs). This enables tests to integrate with the developers' workflows.
- Support unattended test runs for integration with build processes and batch runs. Continuous Integration servers require this.

- Email Notifications (automated notification on failure or threshold levels). This may be the test runner or tooling that executes it.
- Support distributed execution environment (distributed test bed)
- Distributed application support (distributed SUT)

Framework approach in automation

A framework is an integrated system that sets the rules of Automation of a specific product. This system integrates the function libraries, test data sources, object details and various reusable modules. These components act as small building blocks which need to be assembled to represent a business process. The framework provides the basis of test automation and simplifies the automation effort.

There are various types of frameworks. They are categorized on the basis of the automation component they leverage. These are:

1. Data-driven testing
2. Modularity-driven testing
3. Keyword-driven testing
4. Hybrid testing
5. Model-based testing

Popular Test Automation Tools

Tool Name	Company Name	Latest Version
HP QuickTest Professional	HP	11.0
IBM Rational Functional Tester	IBM Rational	8.1.0.3
Parasoft SOAtest	Parasoft	9.0
Rational robot	IBM Rational	2003
Selenium	OpenSource Tool	1.0.6
SilkTest	Micro Focus	2010
TestComplete	SmartBear Software	8.0
TestPartner	Micro Focus	6.3
WATIR	OpenSource Tool	1.6.5

See also

- List of GUI testing tools
- Software testing
- System testing
- Test automation framework
- Unit test

References

[1] Kolawa, Adam; Huizinga, Dorota (2007). *Automated Defect Prevention: Best Practices in Software Management* (http://www.wiley.com/WileyCDA/WileyTitle/productCd-0470042125.html). Wiley-IEEE Computer Society Press. p. 74. ISBN 0470042125. .

[2] Brian Marick. "When Should a Test Be Automated?" (http://www.stickyminds.com/sitewide.asp?Function=edetail&ObjectType=ART&ObjectId=2010). StickyMinds.com. . Retrieved 2009-08-20.

- Elfriede Dustin, et al.: *Automated Software Testing.* Addison Wesley, 1999, ISBN 0-20143-287-0
- Elfriede Dustin, et al.: *Implementing Automated Software Testing.* Addison Wesley, ISBN 978-0321580511
- Mark Fewster & Dorothy Graham (1999). *Software Test Automation.* ACM Press/Addison-Wesley. ISBN 978-0201331400.
- Roman Savenkov: *How to Become a Software Tester.* Roman Savenkov Consulting, 2008, ISBN 978-0-615-23372-7
- Hong Zhu et al. (2008). *AST '08: Proceedings of the 3rd International Workshop on Automation of Software Test* (http://portal.acm.org/citation.cfm?id=1370042#). ACM Press. ISBN 978-1-60558-030-2.

External links

- Automation Myths (http://www.benchmarkqa.com/pdf/papers_automation_myths.pdf) by M. N. Alam
- Generating Test Cases Automatically (http://www.osc-es.de/media/pdf/dSPACENEWS2007-3_TargetLink_EmbeddedTester_en_701.pdf)
- Practical Experience in Automated Testing (http://www.methodsandtools.com/archive/archive.php?id=33)
- Test Automation: Delivering Business Value (http://www.applabs.com/internal/app_whitepaper_test_automation_delivering_business_value_1v00.pdf)
- Test Automation Snake Oil (http://www.satisfice.com/articles/test_automation_snake_oil.pdf) by James Bach
- When Should a Test Be Automated? (http://www.stickyminds.com/r.asp?F=DART_2010) by Brian Marick
- Why Automation Projects Fail (http://martproservice.com/Why_Software_Projects_Fail.pdf) by Art Beall
- Guidelines for Test Automation framework (http://info.allianceglobalservices.com/Portals/30827/docs/test automation framework and guidelines.pdf)
- Advanced Test Automation (http://www.testars.com/docs/5GTA.pdf)

iMacros

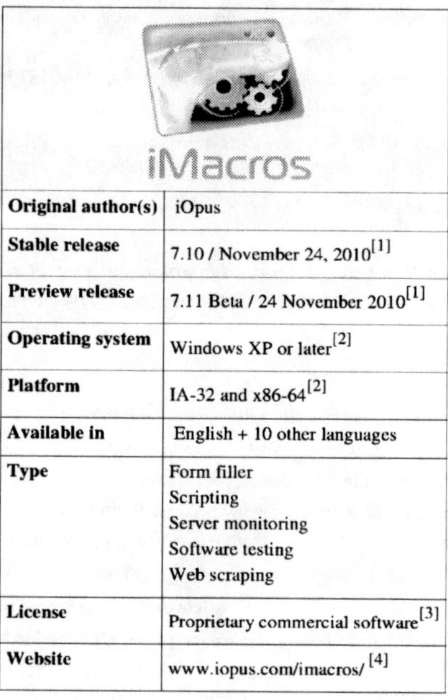

Original author(s)	iOpus
Stable release	7.10 / November 24, 2010[1]
Preview release	7.11 Beta / 24 November 2010[1]
Operating system	Windows XP or later[2]
Platform	IA-32 and x86-64[2]
Available in	English + 10 other languages
Type	Form filler Scripting Server monitoring Software testing Web scraping
License	Proprietary commercial software[3]
Website	www.iopus.com/imacros/ [4]

Stable release	1.1.1 / 8 February 2010[5]
Preview release	3.0.2 Beta / 17 September 2010[5]
Platform	Google Chrome
License	Open-source software[5]

Stable release	7.0.3.0 / November 12, 2010[6]
Platform	Mozilla Firefox
License	Open-source software[3]

Stable release	7.05 / September 2, 2010[1]
Preview release	7.11 Beta / 24 November 2010[1]
Platform	Internet Explorer
License	Freeware[3]

iMacros is an browser extension for the Mozilla Firefox, Google Chrome and Internet Explorer web browsers which adds record and replay functionality similar to that found in web testing and form filler software[7] . The macros can be combined and controlled via Javascript. Demo macros and Javascript code examples are included with the software. iMacros is developed by iOpus. First released in 2001, iMacros was the first macro recorder tool specifically designed and optimized for web browsers [8] and form filling[9] .

iMacros for Firefox and Chrome offer a feature known as social scripting. It allows users to share macros and scripts in a way that is similar to how they share bookmarks on the many social bookmarking websites. After creating a new macro, users can make just one click to share it with their friends as a link, either by distributing the link via email and social bookmarking websites or by embedding it in a website or blog for public access. Technically this is accomplished by embedding the imacro and the controlling Javascript inside a plain text link[10] .

Along with freeware version iMacros is available as a proprietary commercial application[3] with additional features and support for web scripting, web scraping, internet server monitoring and web testing. In addition to working with HTML pages, the commercial editions can automate Adobe Flash, Adobe Flex, Silverlight and Java applets by using Directscreen and image recognition technology.

Advanced versions also contain a command-line interface and application programming interface (API) to automate more complicated tasks and for integration with other programs or scripts. The iMacros API is called Scripting Interface. The Scripting Interface of the iMacros Scripting Edition is designed as a Component Object Model (COM) object and allows the user to remote control (script) the iMacros Browser, Internet Explorer and Firefox web browser from any Windows programming or scripting language.

See also

- List of Firefox extensions

References

[1] "Version History" (http://wiki.imacros.net/Version_History). *iMacros Online Documentation*. iOpus. 12 November 2010. . Retrieved 25 November 2010.

[2] "System requirements" (http://www.iopus.com/imacros/index.htm#sreq). *iMacros | Web Browser Scripting, Data Extraction and Web Testing*. iOpus Inc. . Retrieved 25 November 2010.

[3] "iMacros Feature Comparison - Free and Business Editions" (http://www.iopus.com/imacros/compare/all/). *iMacros website*. iOpus. . Retrieved 25 November 2010.

[4] http://www.iopus.com/imacros/

[5] "iMacros for Chrome § Version History" (http://wiki.imacros.net/iMacros_for_Chrome#Version_History). *iMacros for Chrome Online Documentation*. iOpus. 17 September 2010. . Retrieved 25 November 2010.

[6] "iMacros for Firefox" (https://addons.mozilla.org/en-US/firefox/addon/3863/). *Add-ons for Firefox*. Mozilla Foundation. 11 November 2010. . Retrieved 25 November 2010.

[7] *Firefox 3 Hacks*, O'Reilly, 2008, ISBN978-4-87311-375-3

[8] Goebel, Max et all. *Digging the Wild Web. An Interactive Tool*. Web information systems engineering - WISE 2007: 8th International Conference

[9] Huben, Jan, *Domain Independent Automatic Form Filling*. Web Engineering: 10th International Conference, ICWE 2010, Vienna, Austria

[10] "Automatic Google Search" (http://run.imacros.net/
?code=VkVSU0lPTiBCVUlMRD02MDAwODE0IFJFQ09SREVSPUZYDQpUQUIgVD0xDQpVUkwgR09UTz1odHRwOi8vd3d3Lmdvb2dsZS5jb20vd2ViaHA

aGw9ZW4NClRBRyBQT1M9MSBUWVBFPUlOUFVUOlRFWFQgRk9STT1OQU1FOmYgQVRUUj1OQU1FOnEgQ09OVEVOVD13aWtpcGVkaWE8U1A+

aXM8U1A+
Z3JlYXQNClRBRyBQT1M9MSBUWVBFPUlOUFVUOlNVQk1JVCBGT1JNPU5BTUU6ZiBBVFRSPU5BTUU6YnRuRyYmVkFMVUU6R29vZ2x
Embedded sample imacro. .

External links

- iMacros Consultant (http://forum.iopus.com/viewtopic.php?f=19&t=9692)
- iMacros Forum (http://forum.iopus.com/viewforum.php?f=11)
- Mozilla Firefox Add-on (open source) (https://addons.mozilla.org/en-US/firefox/addon/3863)
- Google Chrome Add-on (open source) (https://chrome.google.com/extensions/detail/deckhobdafgddaglbaokimbcjjdikago)
- iMacros User Manual (Wiki) (http://wiki.imacros.net/iMacros_for_Firefox)
- iMacros Scripts Available For Download (http://www.getimacroscripts.com)

Abnormal end

"Abend" redirects here. For other uses, see the wiktionary box.

An **ABEND** (also ***ab*normal *end*** or **abend**) is an abnormal termination of software, or a program crash.

This usage derives from an error message from the IBM OS/360, IBM zOS operating systems. Usually capitalized, but may appear as "abend". It is humorously claimed to be derived from the German word "Abend" meaning "evening".[1]

Errors or crashes on the Novell NetWare network operating system are usually called ABENDs. Communities of NetWare administrators have sprung up around the Internet, such as abend.org [2].

See also

- Abort
- Programming

References

[1] "Abend" (http://dictionary.die.net/abend) on dictionary.die.net
[2] http://www.abend.org

Anomaly in software

In software testing an **anomaly** is anything that differs from expectation.[1] This expectation can result from many things like from a document (e.g. the expected behaviour is not always written down explicitly, so the developer may implement it differently) or from a person's view (e.g. the person has different opinion regarding usability) or experiences (e.g. the specification is not clear on one thing and the person also knows competitor products, where such a feature is implemented or where the tested software behaves different than these).

An anomaly also can point to a new feature or a usability problem, because the software may be correct with respect to the specification, but has room for improvement.

Another possibility for an anomaly is that a tester executed the test case incorrectly and therefore the expected result is also incorrect (Garbage In, Garbage Out). Some other common terms for software anomalies are: bug, fault, failure, error, defect, problem, deviation, glitch, incident, crash. According to IEEE, the word anomaly should be favored because it has a more neutral meaning.

'Software' in this article is more than just source code.[2] It also refers to: programs, procedures and documentation, and data for the concerning processing on a computer system. Testing software ("testware") is also regarded as software in this context.

The time and place of anomalies can be pretty anywhere in the software development life cycle - it should not be seen from end user perspective only. Most people see anomalies (e.g. failures) during analytical quality assurance measures, but in fact the reason for this anomaly probably occurred earlier. This is why preventive quality assurance are more important: anomalies are found earlier, which can result in lower costs.

Examples for anomalies

- List of notable software bugs
- different screens of death: Screen of Death, Blue Screen of Death
- an anomaly in the game Super Mario Bros.: the Minus World
- in white box testing: data flow anomaly[3] and control flow anomaly
- Easter egg
- buffer overflow, deadlock, division by zero, memory leak, hang (computing)
- more examples you can find in following categories: Category:Computer errors, Category:Programming bugs, Category:Screens of death

See also

- Bug tracking system: the place, where anomalies are collected during software development life cycle
- Issue tracking system: can also used like the bug tracking system, in general used for anomalies by customers
- Crash (computing)
- List of commercial failures in computer and video gaming
- Undocumented feature

References

[1] *IEEE 1044-1993: Standard Classification for Software Anomalies.*, page 1, The Institute of Electrical and Electronics Engineers, Inc., New York, USA, 1994, ISBN 1-55937-383-0
[2] see IEEE 610-1990 and Wikiversity: software testing (http://en.wikiversity.org/wiki/Topic:Software_testing/glossary)
[3] http://en.wikiversity.org/wiki/Topic:Software_testing/design_technique#white_box

External links

- Large database with errors and solutions (http://iderror.com/) A website with a large number of software errors and solutions

C Traps and Pitfalls

C Traps and Pitfalls is a slim computer programming book by former AT&T researcher and programmer Andrew Koenig, its first edition still in print in 2005, which outlines the many ways in which beginners and even sometimes quite experienced C programmers can write poor, malfunctioning and dangerous source code.

It evolved from an earlier technical report, by the same name, published internally at Bell Labs.[1] This, in turn was inspired by a prior paper given by Koenig on "PL/I Traps and Pitfalls" at a SHARE conference in 1977. Koenig wrote that this title was inspired by a 1968 science fiction anthology by Robert Sheckley, "The People Trap and other Pitfalls, Snares, Devices and Delusions, as Well as Two Sniggles and a Contrivance".[2]

References

[1] Koenig, Andrew R., "C Traps and Pitfalls" (http://literateprogramming.com/ctraps.pdf), Bell Telephone Laboratories, Murray Hill, New Jersey, Technical Memorandum.
[2] Cf. Koenig, preface to "C Traps and Pitfalls" book (http://www.acceleratedcpp.com/authors/koenig/bibliography/pitfalls.preface.html).

- Andrew Koenig (1989). C Traps and Pitfalls (http://www.scribd.com/doc/14341289/c-trapspitfalls). Addison-Wesley. ISBN 0-201-17928-8. OCLC 18014955.

Crash (computing)

A **crash** (or **system crash**) in computing is a condition where a computer or a program, either an application or part of the operating system, ceases to function properly, often exiting after encountering errors. When programs freezes or hangs, a crash reporting service documents details of the crash. If the program is a critical part of the operating system kernel, the entire computer may crash. This is different from a hang or freeze where the application or OS continues to run without obvious response to input.

A public payphone that has experienced a fatal error causing a crash and is displaying the Blue Screen of Death.

Many crashes are the result of the execution of a single machine instruction, but the causes of this are many fold. Typical causes are when the program counter is set to an incorrect address or a buffer overflow overwrites a portion of program code due to an earlier bug. In either case, it is quite common for the processor to attempt to execute data or random memory values. Since all data values are possible but only some values are valid instructions, this often results in an illegal instruction exception. By chance such data or random values could be valid (though unplanned) instructions. One might say that the original bug that upset the program counter "caused" the crash, but the actual fault was an illegal instruction some time later. The art of debugging such crashes is connecting the actual cause of the crash (easily determined) with the code that set off the chain of events. This is often very far from obvious—the original bug is usually perfectly valid code from the processor's perspective.

On earlier personal computers, it was actually possible to cause hardware damage through trying to write to hardware addresses outside of the system's main memory. Occasionally, execution of arbitrary data on a system will result in a breakup of screen display. This is widely considered a severe system crash.

Etymology

The term "crash" may originate from the phrase "head crash", which occurs when the read/write heads inside a hard disk physically come into contact with--"crash" into—the platter, the magnetic data storage surface of a hard disk. A head crash is catastrophic to the drive operation, roughly analogous to the severity of a computer crash to computer software.

Application crashes

An application typically crashes when it performs an operation which is not allowed by the operating system. The operating system then triggers an exception or signal in the application. Unix applications traditionally responded to the signal by dumping core. Most Windows and Unix GUI applications respond by displaying a dialog box (such as the one shown to the right) with the option to attach a debugger if one is installed. This behavior is called "crashing". Some applications attempt to recover from the error and continue execution instead of crashing.

An airport display running a program under Windows that has crashed due to a memory read access violation

Typical errors that result in application crashes include:

- attempting to read or write memory that is not allocated for reading or writing by that application *(segmentation fault)* or x86 specific *(general protection fault)*
- attempting to execute privileged or invalid instructions
- attempting to perform I/O operations on hardware devices to which it does not have permission to access
- passing invalid arguments to system calls
- attempting to access other system resources to which the application does not have permission to access *(bus error)*
- attempting to execute machine instructions with bad arguments (depending on CPU architecture): divide by zero, operations on denorms or NaN values, memory access to unaligned addresses, etc.

Website server crashes

The software running the server behind a website may crash, rendering it inaccessible entirely or providing only an error message instead of normal content.

For example: If a site was using a SQL database (such as MySQL) for a script (such as php) and that SQL server crashed, then php would display a connection error.

Operating system crashes

An operating system crash commonly occurs when a hardware exception occurs that cannot be handled. Operating system crashes can also occur when internal sanity-checking logic within the operating system detects that the operating system has lost its internal self-consistency.

Modern multi-tasking operating systems, such as Windows NT, Linux, or Mac OS X usually remain unharmed when an application program crashes.

See also

- Blue Screen of Death
- Crash to Desktop
- Segmentation fault
- Safe Mode
- Debugging
- Kernel panic
- Reboot
- Crash reporter
- Data loss
- SystemRescueCD

Crash to desktop

A **crash to desktop** (or **CTD**) is a computer program crash which is said to occur when a program (commonly a video game) unexpectedly quits, abruptly taking the user back to the desktop. Usually, the term is applied only to crashes where no error is displayed, hence all the user sees as a result of the crash is the desktop. Many times there is no apparent action that causes a CTD. During normal function, the game may freeze for a shorter period of time, and then close by itself. Also during normal function, the game may become a black screen and play the last few seconds of sound (depending on the size of the data buffer) that was being played repeatedly before it crashes to desktop. Other times it may appear to be triggered by a certain action, such as loading an area.

The CTD bugs are considered particularly problematic for users. Since they frequently display no error message, it can be very difficult to track down the source of the problem, especially if the times they occur and the actions taking place right before the CTD do not appear to have any pattern or common ground. One way to track down the source of CTDs for games is to run them in windowed-mode. Windows Vista has a new feature that can help track down the cause of a CTD problem when it occurs on any program. Windows XP also included a similar feature as well.

Some computer programs, such as StepMania and BBC's Bamzooki, also crash to desktop if in full-screen, but displays the error in a separate window when the user has returned to the desktop. Crashes are usually caused by website failure or system failure.

See also

- Crash (computing)
- Software bug
- Blue Screen of Death

Deadlock

A **deadlock** is a situation where in two or more competing actions are each waiting for the other to finish, and thus neither ever does. It is often seen in a paradox like the "chicken or the egg". The concept of a Catch 22 is similar.

> When two trains approach each other at a crossing, both shall come to a full stop and neither shall start up again until the other has gone.
>
> — Illogical statute passed by the Kansas Legislature[1]

In computer science, **Coffman deadlock** refers to a specific condition when two or more processes are each waiting for each other to release a resource, or more than two processes are waiting for resources in a circular chain (see *Necessary conditions*). Deadlock is a common problem in multiprocessing where many processes share a specific type of mutually exclusive resource known as a *software lock* or *soft lock*. Computers intended for the *time-sharing* and/or *real-time* markets are often equipped with a *hardware lock* (or *hard lock*) which guarantees *exclusive access* to processes, forcing serialized access. Deadlocks are particularly troubling because there is no *general* solution to avoid (soft) deadlocks.

This situation may be likened to two people who are drawing diagrams, with only one pencil and one ruler between them. If one person takes the pencil and the other takes the ruler, a deadlock occurs when the person with the pencil needs the ruler and the person with the ruler needs the pencil to finish his work with the ruler. Neither request can be satisfied, so a deadlock occurs.

The telecommunications description of deadlock is weaker than Coffman deadlock because processes can wait for messages instead of resources. Deadlock can be the result of corrupted messages or signals rather than merely waiting for resources. For example, a dataflow element that has been directed to receive input on the wrong link will never proceed even though that link is not involved in a Coffman cycle.

Examples

An example of a deadlock which may occur in database products is the following. Client applications using the database may require exclusive access to a table, and in order to gain exclusive access they ask for a *lock*. If one client application holds a lock on a table and attempts to obtain the lock on a second table that is already held by a second client application, this may lead to deadlock if the second application then attempts to obtain the lock that is held by the first application. (But this particular type of deadlock is easily prevented, e.g., by using an *all-or-none* resource allocation algorithm.)

Another example might be a text formatting program that accepts text sent to it to be processed and then returns the results, but does so only after receiving "enough" text to work on (e.g. 1KB). A text editor program is written that sends the formatter some text and then waits for the results. In this case a deadlock may occur on the last block of text. Since the formatter may not have sufficient text for processing, it will suspend itself while waiting for the additional text, which will never arrive since the text editor has sent it all of the text it has. Meanwhile, the text editor is itself suspended waiting for the last output from the formatter. This type of deadlock is sometimes referred to as a *deadly embrace* (properly used only when only two applications are involved) or *starvation*. However, this situation, too, is easily prevented by having the text editor send a *forcing* message (e.g. EOF, (End Of File)) with its last (partial) block of text, which will *force* the formatter to return the last (partial) block after formatting, and not wait for additional text.

In communications, corrupted messages may cause computers to go into bad states where they are not communicating properly. The network may be said to be deadlocked even though no computer is waiting for a resource. This is different than a Coffman deadlock.

Necessary conditions

There are four necessary and sufficient conditions for a Coffman deadlock to occur, known as the *Coffman conditions* from their first description in a 1971 article by E. G. Coffman.

1. Mutual exclusion condition: a resource that cannot be used by more than one process at a time
2. Hold and wait condition: processes already holding resources may request new resources
3. No preemption condition: No resource can be forcibly removed from a process holding it, resources can be released only by the explicit action of the process.

The first three conditions are necessary but not sufficient for a deadlock to exist. For deadlock to actually take place,a fourth condition is required:

1. Circular wait condition: two or more processes form a circular chain where each process waits for a resource that the next process in the chain holds

Prevention

- Removing the mutual exclusion condition means that no process may have exclusive access to a resource. This proves impossible for resources that cannot be spooled, and even with spooled resources deadlock could still occur. Algorithms that avoid mutual exclusion are called non-blocking synchronization algorithms.
- The "hold and wait" conditions may be removed by requiring processes to request all the resources they will need before starting up (or before embarking upon a particular set of operations); this advance knowledge is frequently difficult to satisfy and, in any case, is an inefficient use of resources. Another way is to require processes to release all their resources before requesting all the resources they will need. This too is often impractical. (Such algorithms, such as serializing tokens, are known as the all-or-none algorithms.)
- A "no preemption" (lockout) condition may also be difficult or impossible to avoid as a process has to be able to have a resource for a certain amount of time, or the processing outcome may be inconsistent or thrashing may occur. However, inability to enforce preemption may interfere with a *priority* algorithm. (Note: Preemption of a "locked out" resource generally implies a rollback, and is to be avoided, since it is very costly in overhead.) Algorithms that allow preemption include lock-free and wait-free algorithms and optimistic concurrency control.
- The circular wait condition: Algorithms that avoid circular waits include "disable interrupts during critical sections", and "use a hierarchy to determine a partial ordering of resources" (where no obvious hierarchy exists, even the memory address of resources has been used to determine ordering) and Dijkstra's solution.

Avoidance

Deadlock can be avoided if certain information about processes is available in advance of resource allocation. For every resource request, the system sees if granting the request will mean that the system will enter an *unsafe* state, meaning a state that could result in deadlock. The system then only grants requests that will lead to *safe* states. In order for the system to be able to figure out whether the next state will be safe or unsafe, it must know in advance at any time the number and type of all resources in existence, available, and requested. One known algorithm that is used for deadlock avoidance is the Banker's algorithm, which requires resource usage limit to be known in advance. However, for many systems it is impossible to know in advance what every process will request. This means that deadlock avoidance is often impossible.

Two other algorithms are Wait/Die and Wound/Wait, each of which uses a symmetry-breaking technique. In both these algorithms there exists an older process (O) and a younger process (Y). Process age can be determined by a timestamp at process creation time. Smaller time stamps are older processes, while larger timestamps represent younger processes.

	Wait/Die	Wound/Wait
O needs a resource held by Y	O waits	Y dies
Y needs a resource held by O	Y dies	Y waits

It is important to note that a process may be in an unsafe state but would not result in a deadlock. The notion of safe/unsafe states only refers to the ability of the system to enter a deadlock state or not. For example, if a process requests A which would result in an unsafe state, but releases B which would prevent circular wait, then the state is unsafe but the system is not in deadlock.

Detection

Often, neither avoidance nor deadlock prevention may be used. Instead deadlock detection and process restart are used by employing an algorithm that tracks resource allocation and process states, and rolls back and restarts one or more of the processes in order to remove the deadlock. Detecting a deadlock that has already occurred is easily possible since the resources that each process has locked and/or currently requested are known to the resource scheduler or OS.

Detecting the possibility of a deadlock *before* it occurs is much more difficult and is, in fact, *generally* undecidable, because the halting problem can be rephrased as a deadlock scenario. However, in *specific* environments, using *specific* means of locking resources, deadlock detection may be *decidable*. In the *general* case, it is not possible to distinguish between algorithms that are merely waiting for a very unlikely set of circumstances to occur and algorithms that will never finish because of deadlock.

Deadlock detection techniques include, but is not limited to, Model checking. This approach constructs a Finite State-model on which it performs a progress analysis and finds all possible terminal sets in the model. These then each represent a deadlock.

Distributed deadlock

Distributed deadlocks can occur in distributed systems when distributed transactions or concurrency control is being used. Distributed deadlocks can be detected either by constructing a global wait-for graph, from local wait-for graphs at a deadlock detector or by a distributed algorithm like edge chasing.

In a Commitment ordering based distributed environment (including the Strong strict two-phase locking (SS2PL, or rigorous) special case) distributed deadlocks are resolved automatically by the atomic commitment protocol (e.g. two-phase commit (2PC)), and no global wait-for graph or other resolution mechanism are needed. Similar automatic global deadlock resolution occurs also in environments that employ 2PL that is not SS2PL (and typically not CO; see *Deadlocks in 2PL*). However 2PL that is not SS2PL is rarely utilized in practice.

Phantom deadlocks are deadlocks that are detected in a distributed system due to system internal delays, but no longer actually exist at the time of detection.

Distributed deadlock prevention

Lets consider the "When two trains approach each other at a crossing" example defined above. Just-in-time Prevention works like having a person standing at the crossing (the crossing guard) with a switch that will let only one train onto "super tracks" which runs above and over the other waiting train(s).

Before we look into threads using Just-in-time Prevention, lets look into the conditions which already exist for regular locking.

- For non-recursive locks, this lock may be entered only once (where a single thread entering twice without unlocking will cause a deadlock, or throw an exception to enforce circular wait prevention).

- For recursive locks, only one thread is allowed to pass through a lock. If any other threads enter the lock, they must wait until the initial thread that passed through completes n number of times it has entered.

So the issue with the first one is it does no deadlock prevention at all. The second doesn't do Distributed deadlock prevention. But the 2nd one is redefined to prevent a deadlock scenario the first one doesn't address. And the only other scenario I am aware of that may cause deadlocks is when two or more lockers lock on each other. So why not expand the definition above one more time?

Well, we can, if we use add a variable to the recursive lock condition which guarantees that at least one thread runs among all locks—distributed deadlock prevention. And just like having a super track in the train example, I use "super thread" in this locking example.

- Recursively, only one thread is allowed to pass through a lock. If other threads enter the lock, they must wait until the initial thread that passed through completes n number of times. But if the number of threads that enter locking equal the number that are locked, assign one thread as the super-thread, and only allow it to run (tracking the number of times it enters/exits locking) until it completes.

After a super-thread is finished, the condition changes back to using the logic from the recursive lock, and the exiting super-thread

1. sets itself as not being a super-thread
2. notifies the locker that other locked, waiting threads need to re-check this condition

If a deadlock scenario exists, set a new super-thread and follow that logic. Otherwise, resume regular locking.

Issues not addressed above

A lot of confusion revolves around the halting problem. But this logic in-no-way solves the halting problem. This is because we know and control the conditions in which locking occurs, giving us a specific solution (instead of the otherwise required general solution the halting problem requires). Still this locker prevents all deadlocked!

Well, it does when only considering locks using this logic. But if it is use with other locking mechanisms, a lock that is started never unlocks (e.g. exception thrown jumping out without unlocking, looping indefinitely within a lock, or coding error forgetting to call unlock), deadlocking is very much possible. And to increase our condition to include these would require solving the halting issue, since we would be dealing with conditions we know nothing about and are unable to change.

Another issue is that this doesn't address the temporary deadlocking issue (not really a deadlock, but a performance killer), where two or more threads lock on each other while another unrelated threads is running. These temporary deadlocks could have a thread running exclusively within them, increasing parallelism. But because of how the distributed deadlock detection works for all locks, and not subsets therein, the unrelated running thread must complete before performing the super-thread logic to remove the temporary deadlock.

I hope you see the temporary live-lock scenario in the above. If another unrelated running thread begins before the first unrelated thread exits, another duration of temporary deadlocking will occur. And if this happens continuously (extremely rare), the temporary deadlock can be extended until right before the program exits, when the other unrelated threads are guaranteed to finish (because of the guarantee that one thread will always run to completion).

Further expansion

This can be further expanded to involve additional logic to increase parallelism where temporary deadlocks might otherwise occur. But for each step of adding more logic, we add more overhead.

A couple of examples include: expanding distributed super-thread locking mechanism to consider each subset of existing locks; Wait-For-Graph (WFG) [2] algorithms, which tracks all cycles that cause deadlocks (including temporary deadlocks); and heuristics algorithms which don't necessarily increase parallelism in 100% of the places that temporary deadlocks are possible, but instead compromise by solving them in enough places that performance/overhead vs parallelism is acceptable (e.g. for each processor available, work towards finding deadlock cycles less than the number of processors + 1 deep).

Livelock

A **livelock** is similar to a deadlock, except that the states of the processes involved in the livelock constantly change with regard to one another, none progressing.[3] Livelock is a special case of resource starvation; the general definition only states that a specific process is not progressing.[4]

A real-world example of livelock occurs when two people meet in a narrow corridor, and each tries to be polite by moving aside to let the other pass, but they end up swaying from side to side without making any progress because they both repeatedly move the same way at the same time.

Livelock is a risk with some algorithms that detect and recover from deadlock. If more than one process takes action, the deadlock detection algorithm can repeatedly trigger. This can be avoided by ensuring that only one process (chosen randomly or by priority) takes action.[5]

See also

- Banker's algorithm
- Catch 22
- Deadlock provision
- Dining philosophers problem
- File locking
- Gridlock (in vehicular traffic)
- Hang
- Impasse
- Infinite loop
- Linearizability
- Model checker can be used to formally verify that a system will never enter a deadlock.
- Ostrich algorithm
- Priority inversion
- Race condition
- Sleeping barber problem
- Stalemate
- Readers-writer lock
- Synchronization

References

[1] A Treasury of Railroad Folklore, B.A. Botkin & A.F. Harlow, p. 381

[2] http://www.cse.scu.edu/~jholliday/dd_9_16.htm

[3] Mogul, Jeffrey C.; K. K. Ramakrishnan (1996). "Eliminating receive livelock in an interrupt-driven kernel" (http://citeseer.ist.psu.edu/326777.html). .

[4] Anderson, James H.; Yong-jik Kim (2001). "Shared-memory mutual exclusion: Major research trends since 1986" (http://citeseer.ist.psu.edu/anderson01sharedmemory.html). .

[5] Zöbel, Dieter (October 1983). "The Deadlock problem: a classifying bibliography" (http://doi.acm.org/10.1145/850752.850753). *ACM SIGOPS Operating Systems Review* **17** (4): 6–15. ISSN 0163-5980. .

Further reading

- Kaveh, Nima; Emmerich, Wolfgang. *Deadlock Detection in Distributed Object Systems* (http://www.cs.ucl.ac.uk/staff/w.emmerich/publications/ESEC01/ModelChecking/esec.pdf). London: University College London.
- Bensalem, Saddek; Fernandez, Jean-Claude; Havelund, Klaus; Mounier, Laurent (2006). "Confirmation of deadlock potentials detected by runtime analysis". *Proceedings of the 2006 workshop on Parallel and distributed systems: Testing and debugging* (ACM): 41–50. doi:10.1145/1147403.1147412.
- Coffman, Edward G., Jr.; Elphick, Michael J.; Shoshani, Arie (1971). "System Deadlocks" (http://www.cs.umass.edu/~mcorner/courses/691J/papers/TS/coffman_deadlocks/coffman_deadlocks.pdf). *ACM Computing Surveys* **3** (2): 67–78. doi:10.1145/356586.356588.
- Mogul, Jeffrey C.; Ramakrishnan, K. K. (1997). "Eliminating receive livelock in an interrupt-driven kernel". *ACM Transactions on Computer Systems* **15** (3): 217–252. doi:10.1145/263326.263335. ISSN 07342071.

- Havender, James W. (1968). "Avoiding deadlock in multitasking systems" (http://domino.research.ibm.com/tchjr/journalindex.nsf/a3807c5b4823c53f85256561006324be/c014b699abf7b9ea85256bfa00685a38?OpenDocument). *IBM Systems Journal* **7** (2): 74.
- Holliday, JoAnne L.; El Abbadi, Amr. "Distributed Deadlock Detection" (http://www.cse.scu.edu/~jholliday/dd_9_16.htm). *Encyclopedia of Distributed Computing* (Kluwer Academic Publishers).
- Knapp, Edgar (1987). "Deadlock detection in distributed databases". *ACM Computing Surveys* **19** (4): 303–328. doi:10.1145/45075.46163. ISSN 03600300.

External links

- " Advanced Synchronization in Java Threads (http://www.onjava.com/pub/a/onjava/2004/10/20/threads2.html)" by Scott Oaks and Henry Wong
- Deadlock Detection Agents (http://www-db.in.tum.de/research/projects/dda.html)
- DeadLock at the Portland Pattern Repository
- Etymology of "Deadlock" (http://www.etymonline.com/index.php?term=deadlock)
- ARCS - A Web Service approach to alleviating deadlock (http://www.arcs.us)
- Non-Hard Locking Read-Write Locker (http://nohardlockrwlocker.codeplex.com/)

Debugger

A **debugger** or **debugging tool** is a computer program that is used to test and debug other programs (the "target" program). The code to be examined might alternatively be running on an *instruction set simulator* (ISS), a technique that allows great power in its ability to halt when specific conditions are encountered but which will typically be somewhat slower than executing the code directly on the appropriate (or the same) processor. Some debuggers offer two modes of operation - full or partial simulation, to limit this impact.

When the program "crashes" or reaches a preset condition, the debugger typically shows the position in the original code if it is a **source-level debugger** or **symbolic debugger**, commonly now seen in integrated development environments. If it is a **low-level debugger** or a **machine-language debugger** it shows the line in the disassembly (unless it also has online access to the original source code and can display the appropriate section of code from the assembly or compilation).(A "crash" happens when the program cannot normally continue because of a programming bug. For example, the program might have tried to use an instruction not available on the current version of the CPU or attempted to access unavailable or protected memory.)

Typically, debuggers also offer more sophisticated functions such as running a program step by step (**single-stepping** or program animation), stopping (**breaking**) (pausing the program to examine the current state) at some event or specified instruction by means of a breakpoint, and tracking the values of some variables. Some debuggers have the ability to modify the state of the program while it is running, rather than merely to observe it. It may also possible to continue execution at a different location in the program to bypass a crash or logical error.

The importance of a good debugger cannot be overstated. Indeed, the existence and quality of such a tool for a given language and platform can often be the deciding factor in its use, even if another language/platform is better-suited to the task.. The absence of a debugger, having once been accustomed to using one, has been said to "make you feel like a blind man in a dark room looking for a black cat that isn't there"[1] . However, software can (and often does) behave differently running under a debugger than normally, due to the inevitable changes the presence of a debugger will make to a software program's internal timing. As a result, even with a good debugging tool, it is often very difficult to track down runtime problems in complex multi-threaded or distributed systems.

The same functionality which makes a debugger useful for eliminating bugs allows it to be used as a software cracking tool to evade copy protection, digital rights management, and other software protection features. It often also makes it useful as a general testing verification tool test coverage and performance analyzer, especially if instruction path lengths are shown.

Most current mainstream debugging engines, such as gdb and dbx provide console-based command line interfaces. Debugger front-ends are popular extensions to debugger engines that provide IDE integration, program animation, and visualization features. Some early mainframe debuggers such as Oliver and SIMON provided this same functionality for the IBM System/360 and later operating systems, as long ago as the 1970s.

Language dependency

Some debuggers operate on a single specific language while others can handle multiple languages transparently. For example if the main target program is written in COBOL but CALLs Assembler subroutines and also PL/1 subroutines, the debugger may dynamically switch modes to accommodate the changes in language as they occur.

Memory protection

Some debuggers also incorporate memory protection to avoid storage violations such as buffer overflow. This may be extremely important in transaction processing environments where memory is dynamically allocated from memory 'pools' on a task by task basis.

Hardware support for debugging

Most modern microprocessors have at least one of these features in their CPU design to make debugging easier:

- hardware support for single-stepping a program, such as the trap flag.
- An instruction set that meets the Popek and Goldberg virtualization requirements makes it easier to write debugger software that runs on the same CPU as the software being debugged; such a CPU can execute the inner loops of the program under test at full speed, and still remain under the control of the debugger.
- In-System Programming allows an external hardware debugger to re-program a system under test (for example, adding or removing instruction breakpoints). Many systems with such ISP support also have other hardware debug support.
- Hardware support for code and data breakpoints, such as address comparators and data value comparators or, with considerably more work involved, page fault hardware.
- JTAG access to hardware debug interfaces such as those on ARM architecture processors or using the Nexus command set. Processors used in embedded systems typically have extensive JTAG debug support.
- Microcontrollers with as few as six pins need to use low pin-count substitutes for JTAG, such as BDM, Spy-Bi-Wire, or DebugWire on the Atmel AVR. DebugWire, for example, uses bidirectional signaling on the RESET pin.

List of debuggers

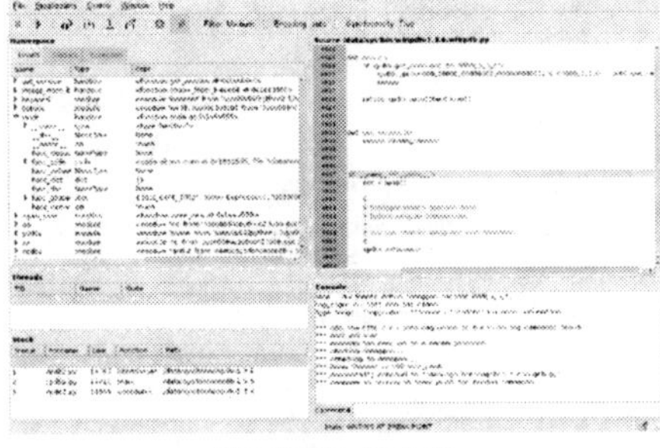
Winpdb debugging itself.

- AppPuncher Debugger — for debugging Rich Internet Applications
- AQtime
- CA/EZTEST — was a CICS interactive test/debug software package
- CharmDebug [2] — a Debugger for Charm++
- CodeView
- DBG — a PHP Debugger and Profiler
- dbx
- DDD (Data Display Debugger)
- Distributed Debugging Tool (Allinea DDT)
- DDTLite — Allinea DDTLite for Visual Studio 2008
- DEBUG — the built-in debugger of DOS and Microsoft Windows
- Debugger for MySQL [3]
- Opera Dragonfly
- Dynamic debugging technique (DDT), and its octal counterpart Octal Debugging Technique
- Eclipse
- Embedded System Debug Plug-in for Eclipse
- FusionDebug
- gDEBugger [4] OpenGL, OpenGL ES and OpenCL Debugger and Profiler. For Windows, Linux, Mac OS X and iPhone
- GNU Debugger (GDB), GNU Binutils
- Intel Debugger (IDB)
- Insight
- Parasoft Insure++
- iSYSTEM — In circuit debugger for Embedded Systems
- Interactive Disassembler (IDA Pro)
- Java Platform Debugger Architecture
- Jinx — a whole-system debugger for heisenbugs. It works transparently as a device driver.
- JSwat — open-source Java debugger
- MacsBug
- Nemiver — graphical C/C++ Debugger for the GNOME desktop environment
- OLIVER (CICS interactive test/debug) - a GUI equipped *instruction set simulator* (ISS)
- OllyDbg
- Omniscient Debugger — Forward and backward debugger for Java
- pydbg
- IBM Rational Purify
- RealView Debugger — Commercial debugger produced for and designed by ARM
- sdb
- SIMMON (Simulation Monitor)
- SIMON (Batch Interactive test/debug) — a GUI equipped *instruction set simulator* (ISS) for batch
- SoftICE
- Software Diagnostics Developer Edition [5]
- TimeMachine — Forward and backward debugger designed by Green Hills Software

- TotalView
- Turbo Debugger
- Ups — C, Fortran source level debugger
- Valgrind
- VB Watch Debugger — debugger for Visual Basic 6.0
- Microsoft Visual Studio Debugger
- WinDbg
- WinGDB [6] — Debugging with GDB under Visual Studio. Remote Linux (via SSH), MinGW, Cygwin, embedded systems.
- Xdebug — PHP debugger and profiler

Debugger front-ends

Some of the most capable and popular debuggers only implement a simple command line interface (CLI) — often to maximize portability and minimize resource consumption. Debugging via a graphical user interface (GUI) can be considered easier and more productive though. This is the reason for GUI debugger front-ends, that allow users to monitor and control subservient CLI-only debuggers via graphical user interface. Some GUI debugger front-ends are designed to be compatible with a variety of CLI-only debuggers, while others are targeted at one specific debugger.

List of debugger front-ends

- Many Integrated development environments come with integrated debuggers (or front-ends to standard debuggers).
  - Many Eclipse perspectives, e.g. the Java Development Tools (JDT) [7], provide a debugger front-end.
- DDD is the standard front-end from the GNU Project. It is a complex tool that works with most common debuggers (GDB, jdb, Python debugger, Perl debugger, Tcl, and others) natively or with some external programs (for PHP).
- GDB (the GNU debugger) GUI
  - Insight [8] — Insight is a graphical user interface to GDB.
  - Emacs — Emacs editor with built in support for the GNU Debugger acts as the frontend.
  - KDbg — Part of the KDE development tools.
  - Nemiver — A GDB frontend that integrates well in the GNOME desktop environment.
  - xxgdb — X-window frontend for GDB and dbx debugger.
  - Qt Creator — multi-platform frontend for GDB (debugging example [9]).
  - cgdb [10] — ncurses terminal program that mimics vim key mapping.
  - ccdebug [11]— A graphical GDB frontend using the Qt toolkit.
  - WinGDB [6] — front-ends GDB under Visual Studio. Remote Linux (via SSH), MinGW, Cygwin, and embedded systems.
  - Padb — has a parallel front-end to GDB allowing it to target parallel applications.
  - Allinea's DDT — a parallel and distributed front-end to a modified version of GDB.
  - Xcode — contains a GDB front-end as well.
  - SlickEdit — contains a GDB front-end as well.
  - Eclipse C/C++ Development Tools (CDT) [12] — includes visual debugging tools based on GDB.

See also

- Anomaly in software
- Breakpoint
- Computer programming
- Core dump
- Debugging
- Kernel debugger
- List of tools for static code analysis
- Memory debugger
- Profiler (computer science)
- Remote debugging
- Software testing

References

- Jonathan B. Rosenberg, How Debuggers Work: Algorithms, Data Structures, and Architecture, John Wiley & Sons, ISBN 0-471-14966-7

[1] http://www.berniecode.com/blog/2007/03/08/how-to-debug-javascript-with-visual-web-developer-express/
[2] http://charm.cs.uiuc.edu/research/parallel_debug/
[3] http://www.mydebugger.com
[4] http://www.gremedy.com/gDEBuggerCL.php
[5] http://www.softwarediagnostics.com
[6] http://www.wingdb.com:
[7] http://www.eclipse.org/jdt/index.php
[8] http://sourceware.org/insight/
[9] http://doc.qt.nokia.com/qtcreator-2.0/creator-debugging-example.html
[10] http://cgdb.sourceforge.net/
[11] http://ccdebug.sourceforge.net/
[12] http://www.eclipse.org/cdt/

External links

- Debugging tools (http://www.dmoz.org//Computers/Programming/Development_Tools/Debugging//) at the Open Directory Project
- Debugging Tools for Windows (http://www.microsoft.com/whdc/devtools/debugging/)
- OpenRCE: Various Debugger Resources and Plug-ins (http://www.openrce.org)
- Parallel computing development and debugging tools (http://www.dmoz.org//Computers/Parallel_Computing/Programming/Tools//) at the Open Directory Project

Division by zero

In mathematics, a division is called a **division by zero** if the divisor (denominator) is zero. Such a division can be formally expressed as $a / 0$ where a is the dividend (numerator). Whether this expression can be assigned a well-defined value depends upon the mathematical setting. In ordinary (real number) arithmetic, the expression has no meaning, as there is no number which, multiplied by 0, gives a ($a \neq 0$).

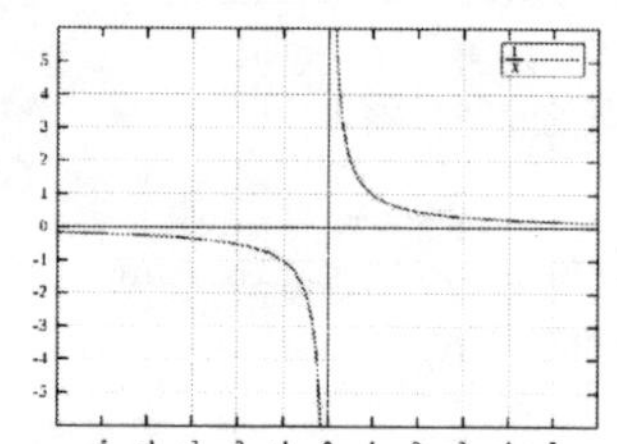

The function $y = 1/x$. As x approaches 0 from the right, y approaches infinity. As x approaches 0 from the left, y approaches minus infinity (see asymptote).

In computer programming, an attempt to divide by zero may, depending on the programming language and the type of number being divided by zero, generate an exception, generate an error message, crash the program being executed, generate either positive or negative infinity, or could result in a special not-a-number value (see below).

Historically, one of the earliest recorded references to the mathematical impossibility of assigning a value to $a / 0$ is contained in George Berkeley's criticism of infinitesimal calculus in *The Analyst*; see Ghosts of departed quantities.

In elementary arithmetic

When division is explained at the elementary arithmetic level, it is often considered as a description of dividing a set of objects into equal parts. As an example, consider having ten apples, and these apples are to be distributed equally to five people at a table. Each person would receive $\frac{10}{5} = 2$ apples. Similarly, if there are 10 apples, and only one person at the table, that person would receive $\frac{10}{1} = 10$ apples. So for dividing by zero – what is the number of apples that each person receives when 10 apples are evenly distributed amongst 0 people? Certain words can be pinpointed in the question to highlight the problem. The problem with this question is the "when". There is no way to distribute 10 apples amongst 0 people. In mathematical jargon, a set of 10 items cannot be partitioned into 0 subsets. So $\frac{10}{0}$, at least in elementary arithmetic, is said to be meaningless, or undefined. Similar problems occur if one has 0 apples and 0 people, but this time the problem is in the phrase "**the** number". A partition is possible (of a set with 0 elements into 0 parts), but since the partition has 0 parts, vacuously every set in our partition has a given number of elements, be it 0, 2, 5, or 1000. If there are, say, 5 apples and 2 people, the problem is in "evenly distribute". In any integer partition of a 5-set into 2 parts, one of the parts of the partition will have more elements than the other. In all of the above three cases, $\frac{10}{0}$, $\frac{0}{0}$ and $\frac{5}{2}$, one is asked to consider an impossible situation before deciding what the answer will be, and that is why the operations are undefined in these cases. To understand division by zero, one must check it with multiplication: multiply the quotient by the divisor to get the original number. However, no number multiplied by zero will produce a product other than zero. To satisfy division by zero, the quotient must be bigger than all other numbers, i.e., infinity. This connection of division by zero to infinity takes us beyond elementary arithmetic (see below). A recurring theme even at this elementary stage is that for every undefined arithmetic operation, there is a corresponding question that is not well-defined. "How many apples will each person receive under a fair distribution of ten apples amongst three people?" is a question that is not well-defined because there can be no fair distribution of ten apples amongst three people. There is another way, however, to explain the division: if one wants to find out how many people, who are satisfied with half an apple, can one satisfy by dividing up one apple, one divides 1 by 0.5. The answer is 2. Similarly, if one wants to know how many people, who are satisfied with nothing, can one satisfy with 1 apple, one divides 1 by 0. The answer is infinite; one can satisfy infinite people, that are satisfied with nothing, with 1 apple. Clearly, one cannot extend the operation of division based on the elementary combinatorial considerations that first define division, but must construct new number systems.

Early attempts

The Brahmasphutasiddhanta of Brahmagupta (598–668) is the earliest known text to treat zero as a number in its own right and to define operations involving zero.[1] The author failed, however, in his attempt to explain division by zero: his definition can be easily proven to lead to algebraic absurdities. According to Brahmagupta,

> A positive or negative number when divided by zero is a fraction with the zero as denominator. Zero divided by a negative or positive number is either zero or is expressed as a fraction with zero as numerator and the finite quantity as denominator. Zero divided by zero is zero.

In 830, Mahavira tried unsuccessfully to correct Brahmagupta's mistake in his book in *Ganita Sara Samgraha*: "A number remains unchanged when divided by zero."[1]

Bhaskara II tried to solve the problem by defining (in modern notation) $\frac{n}{0} = \infty$.[1] This definition makes some sense, as discussed below, but can lead to paradoxes if not treated carefully. These paradoxes were not treated until modern times.

In algebra

It is generally regarded among mathematicians that a natural way to interpret division by zero is to first define division in terms of other arithmetic operations. Under the standard rules for arithmetic on integers, rational numbers, real numbers, and complex numbers, division by zero is undefined. Division by zero must be left undefined in any mathematical system that obeys the axioms of a field. The reason is that division is defined to be the inverse operation of multiplication. This means that the value of a/b is the solution x of the equation $bx = a$ whenever such a value exists and is unique. Otherwise the value is left undefined.

For $b = 0$, the equation $bx = a$ can be rewritten as $0x = a$ or simply $0 = a$. Thus, in this case, the equation $bx = a$ has *no solution* if a is not equal to 0, and has *any* x as a solution if a equals 0. In either case, there is no unique value, so $\frac{a}{b}$is undefined. Conversely, in a field, the expression $\frac{a}{b}$is *always* defined if b is not equal to zero.

Division as the inverse of multiplication

The concept that explains division in algebra is that it is the inverse of multiplication. For example,

$$\frac{6}{3} = 2$$

since 2 is the value for which the unknown quantity in

$$? \times 3 = 6$$

is true. But the expression

$$\frac{6}{0} = ?$$

requires a value to be found for the unknown quantity in

$$? \times 0 = 6.$$

But any number multiplied by 0 is 0 and so there is no number that solves the equation.

The expression

$$\frac{0}{0} = ?$$

requires a value to be found for the unknown quantity in

$$? \times 0 = 0.$$

Again, any number multiplied by 0 is 0 and so this time every number solves the equation instead of there being a single number that can be taken as the value of 0/0.

In general, a single value can't be assigned to a fraction where the denominator is 0 so the value remains undefined (see below for other applications).

Fallacies based on division by zero

It is possible to disguise a special case of division by zero in an algebraic argument,[1] leading to spurious proofs that 1 = 2 such as the following:

With the following assumptions:

$$0 \times 1 = 0$$

$$0 \times 2 = 0.$$

The following must be true:

$$0 \times 1 = 0 \times 2.$$

Dividing by zero gives:

$$\tfrac{0}{0} \times 1 = \tfrac{0}{0} \times 2.$$

Simplified, yields:

$$1 = 2.$$

The fallacy is the implicit assumption that dividing by 0 is a legitimate operation.

In calculus

Extended real line

At first glance it seems possible to define $a/0$ by considering the limit of a/b as b approaches 0.

For any positive a, the limit from the right is

$$\lim_{b \to 0+} \frac{a}{b} = +\infty$$

however, the limit from the left is

$$\lim_{b \to 0-} \frac{a}{b} = -\infty$$

and so the $\lim_{b \to 0} \frac{a}{b}$ is undefined (the limit is also undefined for negative a).

Furthermore, there is no obvious definition of 0/0 that can be derived from considering the limit of a ratio. The limit

$$\lim_{(a,b) \to (0,0)} \frac{a}{b}$$

does not exist. Limits of the form

$$\lim_{x \to 0} \frac{f(x)}{g(x)}$$

in which both $f(x)$ and $g(x)$ approach 0 as x approaches 0, may equal any real or infinite value, or may not exist at all, depending on the particular functions f and g (see l'Hôpital's rule for discussion and examples of limits of ratios). These and other similar facts show that the expression 0/0 cannot be well-defined as a limit.

Formal operations

A formal calculation is one carried out using rules of arithmetic, without consideration of whether the result of the calculation is well-defined. Thus, it is sometimes useful to think of $a/0$, where $a \neq 0$, as being ∞. This infinity can be either positive, negative, or unsigned, depending on context. For example, formally:

$$\lim_{x\to 0} \frac{1}{x} = \frac{\lim\limits_{x\to 0} 1}{\lim\limits_{x\to 0} x} = \frac{1}{0} = \infty.$$

As with any formal calculation, invalid results may be obtained. A logically rigorous as opposed to formal computation would say only that

$$\lim_{x\to 0+} \frac{1}{x} = \frac{1}{0+} = +\infty \text{ and } \lim_{x\to 0-} \frac{1}{x} = \frac{1}{0-} = -\infty.$$

(Since the one-sided limits are different, the two-sided limit does not exist in the standard framework of the real numbers. Also, the fraction 1/0 is left undefined in the extended real line, therefore it and

$$\frac{\lim\limits_{x\to 0} 1}{\lim\limits_{x\to 0} x}$$

are meaningless expressions.)

Real projective line

The set $\mathbb{R} \cup \{\infty\}$ is the real projective line, which is a one-point compactification of the real line. Here ∞ means an *unsigned infinity*, an infinite quantity that is neither positive nor negative. This quantity satisfies $-\infty = \infty$, which is necessary in this context. In this structure, $a/0 = \infty$ can be defined for nonzero a, and $a/\infty = 0$. It is the natural way to view the range of the tangent and cotangent functions of trigonometry: tan(x) approaches the single point at infinity as x approaches either $+\pi/2$or $-\pi/2$from either direction.

This definition leads to many interesting results. However, the resulting algebraic structure is not a field, and should not be expected to behave like one. For example, $\infty + \infty$ is undefined in the projective line.

Riemann sphere

The set $\mathbb{C} \cup \{\infty\}$ is the Riemann sphere, which is of major importance in complex analysis. Here too ∞ is an unsigned infinity – or, as it is often called in this context, the point at infinity. This set is analogous to the real projective line, except that it is based on the field of complex numbers. In the Riemann sphere, $1/0 = \infty$, but 0/0 is undefined, as is $0 \times \infty$.

Extended non-negative real number line

The negative real numbers can be discarded, and infinity introduced, leading to the set [0, ∞], where division by zero can be naturally defined as $a/0 = \infty$ for positive a. While this makes division defined in more cases than usual, subtraction is instead left undefined in many cases, because there are no negative numbers.

In higher mathematics

Although division by zero cannot be sensibly defined with real numbers and integers, it is possible to consistently define it, or similar operations, in other mathematical structures.

Non-standard analysis

In the hyperreal numbers and the surreal numbers, division by zero is still impossible, but division by non-zero infinitesimals is possible.

Distribution theory

In distribution theory one can extend the function $\frac{1}{x}$ to a distribution on the whole space of real numbers (in effect by using Cauchy principal values). It does not, however, make sense to ask for a 'value' of this distribution at $x = 0$; a sophisticated answer refers to the singular support of the distribution.

Linear algebra

In matrix algebra (or linear algebra in general), one can define a pseudo-division, by setting $a/b = ab^+$, in which b^+ represents the pseudoinverse of b. It can be proven that if b^{-1} exists, then $b^+ = b^{-1}$. If b equals 0, then $0^+ = 0$; see Generalized inverse.

Abstract algebra

Any number system that forms a commutative ring — for instance, the integers, the real numbers, and the complex numbers — can be extended to a wheel in which division by zero is always possible; however, in such a case, "division" has a slightly different meaning.

The concepts applied to standard arithmetic are similar to those in more general algebraic structures, such as rings and fields. In a field, every nonzero element is invertible under multiplication; as above, division poses problems only when attempting to divide by zero. This is likewise true in a skew field (which for this reason is called a division ring). However, in other rings, division by nonzero elements may also pose problems. For example, the ring **Z**/6**Z** of integers mod 6. The meaning of the expression $\frac{2}{2}$ should be the solution x of the equation $2x = 2$. But in the ring **Z**/6**Z**, 2 is not invertible under multiplication. This equation has two distinct solutions, $x = 1$ and $x = 4$, so the expression $\frac{2}{2}$ is undefined.

In field theory, the expression $\frac{a}{b}$ is only shorthand for the formal expression ab^{-1}, where b^{-1} is the multiplicative inverse of b. Since the field axioms only guarantee the existence of such inverses for nonzero elements, this expression has no meaning when b is zero. Modern texts include the axiom $0 \neq 1$ to avoid having to consider the trivial ring or a "field with one element", where the multiplicative identity coincides with the additive identity.

In computer arithmetic

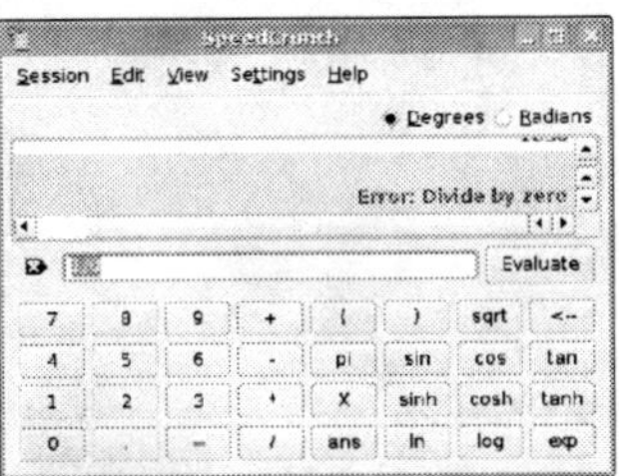

In the SpeedCrunch calculator application, when a number is divided by zero the answer box displays "Error: Divide by zero".

The IEEE floating-point standard, supported by almost all modern floating-point units, specifies that every floating point arithmetic operation, including division by zero, has a well-defined result. The standard supports signed zero, as well as infinity and NaN (*not a number*). There are two zeroes, +0 (*positive zero*) and −0 (*negative zero*) and this removes any ambiguity when dividing. In IEEE 754 arithmetic, $a \div +0$ is positive infinity when a is positive, negative infinity when a is negative, and NaN when $a = \pm 0$. The infinity signs change when dividing by −0 instead.

Integer division by zero is usually handled differently from floating point since there is no integer representation for the result. Some processors generate an exception when an attempt is made to divide an integer by zero, although others will simply continue and generate an incorrect result for the division. The result depends on how division is implemented, and can either be zero, or sometimes the largest possible integer.

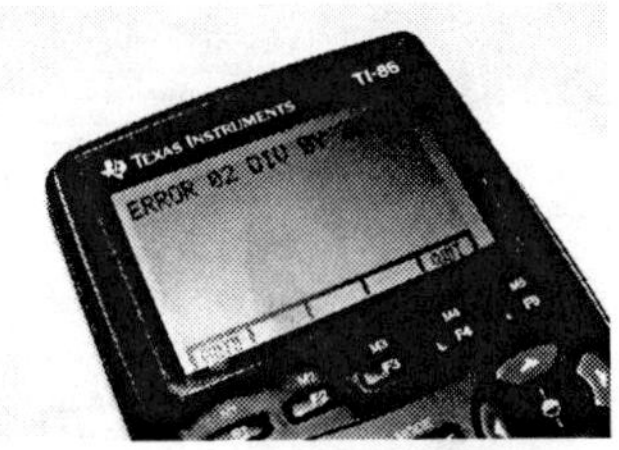

Most calculators, such as this Texas Instruments TI-86, will halt execution and display an error message when the user or a running program attempts to divide by zero.

Because of the improper algebraic results of assigning any value to division by zero, many computer programming languages (including those used by calculators) explicitly forbid the execution of the operation and may prematurely halt a program that attempts it, sometimes reporting a "Divide by zero" error. In these cases, if some special behavior is desired for division by zero, the condition must be explicitly tested (for example, using an if statement). Some programs (especially those that use fixed-point arithmetic where no dedicated floating-point hardware is available) will use behavior similar to the IEEE standard, using large positive and negative numbers to approximate infinities. In some programming languages, an attempt to divide by zero results in undefined behavior.

In two's complement arithmetic, attempts to divide the smallest signed integer by -1 are attended by similar problems, and are handled with the same range of solutions, from explicit error conditions to undefined behavior.

Most calculators will either return an error or state that 1/0 is undefined, however some TI and HP graphing calculators will evaluate $(1/0)^2$ to ∞.

More advanced computer algebra systems will return an infinity as a result for division by zero; for instance, Microsoft Math and Mathematica will show an *ComplexInfinity* result.

Historical accidents

- On September 21, 1997, a divide by zero error on board the USS *Yorktown* (CG-48) *Remote Data Base Manager* brought down all the machines on the network, causing the ship's propulsion system to fail.[2]

See also

- Asymptote
- Defined and undefined
- Indeterminate form
- Zero divisor
- Zeroth

Footnotes

[1] Kaplan, Robert (1999). *The nothing that is: A natural history of zero*. New York: Oxford University Press. pp. 68–75. ISBN 0195142373.
[2] "Sunk by Windows NT" (http://www.wired.com/news/technology/0,1282,13987,00.html). *Wired News*. 1998-07-24. .

References

- Patrick Suppes 1957 (1999 Dover edition), *Introduction to Logic*, Dover Publications, Inc., Mineola, New York. ISBN 0-486-40687-3 (pbk.). This book is in print and readily available. Suppes's §8.5 **The Problem of Division by Zero** begins this way: "That everything is not for the best in this best of all possible worlds, even in mathematics, is well illustrated by the vexing problem of defining the operation of division in the elementary theory of arithmetic" (p. 163). In his §8.7 **Five Approaches to Division by Zero** he remarks that "...there is no uniformly satisfactory solution" (p. 166)
- Charles Seife 2000, *Zero: The Biography of a Dangerous Idea*, Penguin Books, NY, ISBN 0 14 02.9647 6 (pbk.). This award-winning book is very accessible. Along with the fascinating history of (for some) an abhorent notion and others a cultural asset, describes how zero is misapplied with respect to multiplication and division.
- Alfred Tarski 1941 (1995 Dover edition), *Introduction to Logic and to the Methodology of Deductive Sciences*, Dover Publications, Inc., Mineola, New York. ISBN 0-486-28462-X (pbk.). Tarski's §53 **Definitions whose definiendum contains the identity sign** discusses how mistakes are made (at least with respect to zero). He ends his chapter "(A discussion of this rather difficult problem [exactly one number satisfying a definiens] will be omitted here.*)" (p. 183). The * points to Exercise #24 (p. 189) wherein he asks for a proof of the following: "In section 53, the definition of the number '0' was stated by way of an example. To be certain this definition does not lead to a contradiction, it should be preceded by the following theorem: *There exists exactly one number x such that, for any number y, one has: y + x = y*"

Further reading

- Jakub Czajko (July 2004) "On Cantorian spacetime over number systems with division by zero (doi:10.1016/j.chaos.2003.12.046)", *Chaos, Solitons and Fractals*, volume 21, number 2, pages 261–271.
- Ben Goldacre (2006-12-07). "Maths Professor Divides By Zero, Says BBC" (http://www.badscience.net/?p=335).
- To Continue with Continuity (http://www.metaphysica.de/texte/mp2005_2-Cooke.pdf) *Metaphysica* 6, pp. 91–109, a philosophy paper from 2005, reintroduced the (ancient Indian) idea of an applicable whole number equal to 1/0, in a more modern (Cantorian) style.

Easter egg (media)

A virtual **Easter egg** is an intentional hidden message, in-joke or feature in an object such as a movie, book, CD, DVD, computer program, web page or video game. The term was coined—according to Warren Robinett—by Atari after they were pointed to the secret message left by Robinett in the game *Adventure*.[1] It draws a parallel with the custom of the Easter egg hunt observed in many Western nations as well as the last Russian imperial family's tradition of giving elaborately jeweled egg-shaped creations by Carl Fabergé which contained hidden surprises.[2]

This practice is similar in some respects to hidden signature motifs such as Diego Rivera including himself in his murals, Alfred Hitchcock's legendary cameo appearances, and various "Hidden Mickeys" that can be found throughout the various Disney Parks. An early example of this kind of "Easter egg" is Al Hirschfeld's "Nina".

Atari's *Adventure*, released in 1979, contained what was thought to be the first video game "Easter egg", the name of the programmer (Warren Robinett). However, evidence of earlier Easter eggs has since surfaced. Several cartridges for the Fairchild Channel F include previously unknown Easter eggs, programmed by Michael Glass and Brad Reid-Selth, that are believed to predate Robinett's work.[3] [4]

Computer-related Easter eggs

Software-based

Easter eggs are messages, videos, graphics, sound effects, or an unusual change in program behavior that sometimes occur in a software program in response to some undocumented set of commands, mouse clicks, keystrokes or other stimuli intended as a joke or to display program credits.

Easter eggs found in some Unix operating systems caused them to respond to the command "make love" with "not war?" and "why" with "why not" (a reference to *The Prisoner* in Berkeley Unix 1977). The TOPS-10 operating system (for the DEC PDP-10 computer) had the "make love" hack before 1971; it included a short, thoughtful pause before the response. This same behavior occurred on the RSTS/E operating system where the command "make" was used to invoke the TECO editor, and TECO would also provide this response.

Many personal computers have much more elaborate eggs hidden in ROM, including lists of the developers' names, political exhortations, snatches of music, and (in one case) images of the entire development team. Easter eggs in the 1997 version of Microsoft Office include a hidden flight simulator in Microsoft Excel and a pinball game in Microsoft Word (see Easter eggs in Microsoft products).

The Debian GNU/Linux package tool apt-get has an Easter egg involving an ASCII cow when variants on "apt-get moo" are typed into the shell.[5]

VLC media player contains an Easter egg which changes the VLC traffic cone logo so that it's wearing a Santa hat. The logo changes on December 18, one week before Christmas, and reverts to its normal appearance on January 1.

Screenshot of Stickies' (version 1.0.4 for Mac OS 9) Easter egg. The Easter Egg is shown by typing `Antler!` and pressing return

An Easter egg is found on all Microsoft Windows operating systems prior to XP. In the 3D Text screen saver, entering the text "volcano" will display the names of all the volcanoes in the United States. Microsoft removed this Easter egg in XP but added others. One which continues still in Windows XP is to simultaneously hold <Alt>, <Shift>, and the number 2 key in the Solitaire game to produce a forced win.[6]

Microsoft Excel 95 contained a hidden *Doom*-like action game called *The Hall of Tortured Souls*.[7]

Some computer and video game secret levels are triggered by an Easter egg. In 1994's video game *Maniac Mansion: Day of the Tentacle*, a highly acclaimed video game developed by George Lucas's LucasArts, the original prequel Maniac Mansion from 1987 can be played in its full version by using an Arcade game machine in one character's room.

In *Saints Row 2*, there are many known Easter eggs, one of which is a purple Easter bunny rising out of the water.

An example of a recent computer game that features Easter eggs is the Nancy Drew computer games made by Her Interactive.

Google Maps contains several Easter eggs whereby a user asking for directions from Japan to China, from New York to Tokyo, or from Taiwan to China would be directed to either jetski, kayak, or swim across the Pacific Ocean.[8]

Non-software

While computer-related Easter eggs are often found in software, occasionally they exist in hardware or firmware of certain devices. On some home computers, the BIOS ROM contains Easter eggs. Notable examples include several early Apple Macintosh models which had pictures of the development team in the ROM (accessible by pressing the programmer's switch and jumping to a specific memory address, or other equally obscure means), and some errant 1993 AMI BIOS that on 13 November proceeded to play "Happy Birthday" via the PC speaker over and over again instead of booting. Similarly, the Radio Shack Color Computer 3's ROM contained code which would display the likenesses of three Microware developers on a <Ctrl><Alt><Reset> keypress sequence—a hard reset which would discard any information currently in the dynamic memory.[9]

Several oscilloscopes have contained Easter eggs. One example is the HP 54622D, known to have an *Asteroids* clone (and even to save high scores in NV-RAM). Another is the Tektronix 1755A Vector and Waveform Monitor which displays swimming fish when Remote>Software version are selected on the CONFIG menu.

The Commodore Amiga 1000 computer included the signatures of the design and development team embossed on the inside of the case, including Jay Miner and the paw print of his dog Mitchy.[10]

Chip and printed circuit board Easter eggs

Many integrated circuit (chip) designers have included *hidden artwork*, including assorted images, phrases, developer initials, logos, and so on. This artwork, like the rest of the chip, is reproduced in each copy by lithography and etching. These are visible only when the chip package is opened and examined under magnification, so they are, in a sense, more of an "inside joke" than most of the Easter eggs included in software.

The Commodore Amiga models 500, 600 and 1200 each featured Easter eggs, in the form of titles of songs by The B-52's as white printing on the motherboards. The 500 says "B52/Rock Lobster", the 600 says "June Bug", and the 1200 says "Channel Z".[11] The Amiga OS software includes a variety of hidden messages as well.

Easter eggs on DVDs

Easter eggs are also found on movie DVDs. In some cases, an extra click to the right or left, or going up in the menu instead of going down to select a choice will bring up a hidden feature (usually a random object on screen will be highlighted for selection), including concept art, humorous outtakes, or deleted scenes.[12]

Security concerns

Because of the increase in malware, many companies and government offices forbid the use of software containing Easter eggs for security reasons. With the rise of cybercrime and the prevalence of the Easter egg's "cousin", the logic bomb, there is now concern that if the programmer could slip in undocumented code, then the software cannot be trusted. This is of particular concern in offices where personal or confidential information is stored, making it sensitive to theft and ransom. For this reason, many developers have stopped the practice of adding Easter eggs to their software. Microsoft, who has in the past created some of the largest and most elaborate Easter eggs such as the ones in Microsoft Office, no longer allows Easter eggs in their software as part of their Trustworthy Computing initiative.[13]

Douglas W. Jones says that "some Easter eggs may be intentional tools used to detect illegal copying, others are clearly examples of unauthorized functionality that has slipped through the quality-control tests at the vendor." While hidden Easter eggs themselves are harmless, it may be possible for malware to be hidden in similar ways in voting machines or other computers.[14]

See also

- Hidden track
- Undocumented feature
- Easter eggs in Microsoft products
- The Book of Mozilla

Notes

[1] Robinett, Warren: Adventure as a Video Game. Adventure for the Atari 2600. In: Katie Salen a. Eric Zimmerman (eds.): The Game Design Reader. A Rules of the Play Anthology. MIT Press 2006, p. 690–713 (here p. 713) ISBN 0262195364

[2] Hidden DVD Easter Eggs (http://www.hiddendvdEastereggs.com/)

[3] The Very First Easter Egg (Was Not Adventure) (http://atariage.com/forums/index.php?showtopic=59087)

[4] Channel F (http://www.atariage.com/forums/index.php?showtopic=59248&st=50)

[5] "apt-0.6.46.2/cmdline/apt-get.cc:2368" (http://www.google.com/codesearch/p?hl=en#u_CbvX6xxA8/apt-0.6.46.2/cmdline/apt-get.cc&q=apt-get cow&l=2368). .

[6] David Hoye (March 13, 2003), 'Easter egg' hunts can turn up surprises (http://nl.newsbank.com/nl-search/we/Archives?p_product=SB&p_theme=sb&p_action=search&p_maxdocs=200&p_topdoc=1&p_text_direct-0=0F9C5967DFAD25DD&p_field_direct-0=document_id&p_perpage=10&p_sort=YMD_date:D&s_trackval=GooglePM)" (subscription required). *The Sacramento Bee*.

[7] John Gaskell (1999-07-19). "Excel Easter Egg – Excel 95 Hall of Tortured Souls" (http://www.eeggs.com/items/719.html). . Retrieved 30 April 2009.

[8] Firth, Niall (29 October 2010). "How do I get to China? Jet ski! Google Maps joke gives users unorthodox instructions for crossing the Pacific" (http://www.dailymail.co.uk/sciencetech/article-1324917/Google-Maps-joke-gives-users-unorthodox-instructions-crossing-Pacific.html). *The Daily Mail*. . Retrieved 29 October 2010.

[9] TRS-80 CoCo Wiki (http://www.coco25.com/wiki/index.php/CoCo3_Easter_Egg) on the "3 Mugateers" ROM bitmap.

[10] Corrigan, Patricia (2007). *Bringing Science to Life:* A Guide from the Saint Louis Science Center. *Reedy Press. p. 69.*

[11] *Compute* (Small System Service) **12** (6-9). 1990.

[12] "DVD Easter Eggs – Hidden Features on DVDs" (http://www.dvdEastereggs.com/faq.php). *DVD Easter Eggs*. . Retrieved March 22, 2008.

[13] Larry Osterman (October 21, 2005). "Why no Easter Eggs?" (http://blogs.msdn.com/larryosterman/archive/2005/10/21/483608.aspx). *Larry Osterman's WebLog*. MSDN Blogs. . Retrieved 2006-07-29.

[14] "A Conversation with Douglas W. Jones and Peter G. Neumann" (http://queue.acm.org/detail.cfm?id=1180188) 2006

External links

- Easter eggs and the Trusted Computing Base (http://www.networkworld.com/newsletters/sec/0327sec1.html) – Network World article outlining the concern over Easter eggs
- Chip Fun: Microchip-based Easter eggs (http://smithsonianchips.si.edu/chipfun/graff.htm) – From the National Museum of American History; photos by Integrated Circuit Engineering Corp.
- Digital Press Easter eggs (http://www.digitpress.com/eastereggs/) – covering all classic video game systems.
- Lee's PeeknPoke Issue 5 (http://peeknpoke.gazaxian.com/downloads/PeeknPoke_issue5.pdf) – PDF retro game magazine with Atari 2600 hidden Easter egg feature
- Russian based Easter eggs (http://www.Eastereggs.narod.ru) – Russian based Easter eggs

Exception handling

Exception handling is a programming language construct or computer hardware mechanism designed to handle the occurrence of **exceptions**, special conditions that change the normal flow of program execution.

Programming languages differ considerably in their support for exception handling (as distinct from error checking, which is normal program flow that codes for responses to adverse contingencies such as invalid state changes or the unsuccessful termination of invoked operations.) In some programming languages there are functions which cannot be safely called on invalid input data ... or functions which return values which cannot be distinguished from exceptions—for example, in C the *atoi* (ASCII to integer conversion) function may return 0 (zero) for any input that cannot be parsed into a valid value. In such languages the programmer must either perform error checking (possibly through some auxiliary global variable such as C's errno) or input validation (perhaps using regular expressions).

The degree to which such explicit validation and error checking is necessary is in contrast to exception handling support provided by any given programming environment. Hardware exception handling differs somewhat from the support provided by software tools, but similar concepts and terminology are prevalent.

In general, an exception is *handled* (resolved) by saving the current state of execution in a predefined place and switching the execution to a specific subroutine known as an *exception handler*. Depending on the situation, the handler may later resume the execution at the original location using the saved information. For example, a page fault will usually allow the program to be resumed, while a division by zero might not be resolvable transparently.

From the processing point of view, hardware interrupts are similar to resume-able exceptions, though they are typically unrelated to the user's program flow.

From the point of view of the author of a routine, raising an exception is a useful way to signal that a routine could not execute normally. For example, when an input argument is invalid (e.g. a zero denominator in division) or when a resource it relies on is unavailable (like a missing file, or a hard disk error). In systems without exceptions, routines would need to return some special error code. However, this is sometimes complicated by the semipredicate problem, in which users of the routine need to write extra code to distinguish normal return values from erroneous ones.

In runtime engine environments such as Java or .NET, there exist tools that attach to the runtime engine and every time that an exception of interest occurs, they record debugging information that existed in memory at the time the exception was thrown (call stack and heap values). These tools are called automated exception handling or error interception tools and provide 'root-cause' information for exceptions.

Contemporary applications face many design challenges when considering exception handling strategies. Particularly in modern enterprise level applications, exceptions must often cross process boundaries and machine boundaries. Part of designing a solid exception handling strategy is recognizing when a process has failed to the point where it cannot be economically handled by the software portion of the process.[1]

Exception safety

A piece of code is said to be **exception-safe**, if run-time failures within the code will not produce ill effects, such as memory leaks, garbled stored data, or invalid output. Exception-safe code must satisfy invariants placed on the code even if exceptions occur. There are several levels of exception safety:

1. **Failure transparency**, also known as the **no throw guarantee**: Operations are guaranteed to succeed and satisfy all requirements even in presence of exceptional situations. If an exception occurs, it will not throw the exception further up. (Best level of exception safety.)
2. **Commit or rollback semantics**, also known as **strong exception safety** or **no-change guarantee**: Operations can fail, but failed operations are guaranteed to have no side effects so all data retain original values.[2]
3. **Basic exception safety**: Partial execution of failed operations can cause side effects, but invariants on the state are preserved. Any stored data will contain valid values even if data has different values now from before the exception.
4. **Minimal exception safety** also known as **no-leak guarantee**: Partial execution of failed operations may store invalid data but will not cause a crash, and no resources get leaked.
5. **No exception safety**: No guarantees are made. (Worst level of exception safety)

For instance, consider a smart vector type, such as C++'s std::vector or Java's ArrayList. When an item *x* is added to a vector *v*, the vector must actually add *x* to the internal list of objects and also update a count field that says how many objects are in *v*. It may also need to allocate new memory if the existing capacity isn't large enough. This memory allocation may fail and throw an exception. Because of this, a vector that provides failure transparency would be very difficult or impossible to write. However, the vector may be able to offer the strong exception guarantee fairly easily; in this case, either the insertion of *x* into *v* will succeed, or *v* will remain unchanged. If the vector provides only the basic exception safety guarantee, if the insertion fails, *v* may or may not contain *x*, but at least it will be in a consistent state. However, if the vector makes only the minimal guarantee, it's possible that the vector may be invalid. For instance, perhaps the size field of *v* was incremented but *x* wasn't actually inserted, making the state inconsistent. Of course, with no guarantee, the program may crash; perhaps the vector needed to expand but couldn't allocate the memory and blindly ploughs ahead as if the allocation succeeded, touching memory at an invalid address.

Usually at least basic exception safety is required. Failure transparency is difficult to implement, and is usually not possible in libraries where complete knowledge of the application is not available.

Verification of exception handling

The point of exception handling routines is to ensure that the code can handle error conditions. In order to establish that exception handling routines are sufficiently robust, it is necessary to present the code with a wide spectrum of invalid or unexpected inputs, such as can be created via software fault injection and mutation testing (which is also sometimes referred to as fuzz testing). One of the most difficult types of software for which to write exception handling routines is protocol software, since a robust protocol implementation must be prepared to receive input that does not comply with the relevant specification(s).

In order to ensure that meaningful regression analysis can be conducted throughout a software development lifecycle process, any exception handling verification should be highly automated, and the test cases must be generated in a scientific, repeatable fashion. Several commercially available systems exist that perform such testing.

Exception support in programming languages

Many computer languages, such as Actionscript, Ada, BlitzMax, C++, C#, D, ECMAScript, Eiffel, Java, ML, Object Pascal (e.g. Delphi, Free Pascal, and the like), Objective-C, Ocaml, PHP (as of version 5), PL/1, Prolog, Python, REALbasic, Ruby, Visual Prolog and most .NET languages have built-in support for exceptions and exception handling. In those languages, the event of an exception (more precisely, an exception handled by the language) searches back through the stack of function calls until an exception handler is found, with some languages calling for unwinding the stack as the search progresses. That is, if function *f* contains a handler *H* for exception *E*, calls function *g*, which in turn calls function *h*, and an exception *E* occurs in *h*, then functions *h* and *g* may be terminated, and *H* in *f* will handle *E*. An exception-handling language for which this is not true is Common Lisp with its Condition System. Common Lisp calls the exception handler and does not unwind the stack. This allows to continue the computation at exactly the same place where the error occurred (for example when a previously missing file is now available). Mythryl's stackless implementation supports constant-time exception handling without stack unwinding.

Excluding minor syntactic differences, there are only a couple of exception handling styles in use. In the most popular style, an exception is initiated by a special statement (throw, or raise) with an exception object (e.g. with Java or Object Pascal) or a value of a special extendable enumerated type (e.g. with Ada). The scope for exception handlers starts with a marker clause (try, or the language's block starter such as begin) and ends in the start of the first handler clause (catch, except, rescue). Several handler clauses can follow, and each can specify which exception types it handles and what name it uses for the exception object. A few languages also permit a clause (else) that is used in case no exception occurred before the end of the handler's scope was reached. More common is a related clause (finally, or ensure) that is executed whether an exception occurred or not, typically to release resources acquired within the body of the exception-handling block. Notably, C++ does not need and does not provide this construct, and the Resource-Acquisition-Is-Initialization technique should be used to free such resources instead.[3] In its whole, exception handling code might look like this (in Java-like pseudocode; note that an exception type called EmptyLineException would need to be declared somewhere):

```
try {
    line = console.readLine();
    if (line.length() == 0) {
        throw new EmptyLineException("The line read from console
was empty!");
    }
    console.printLine("Hello %s!" % line);
    console.printLine("The program ran successfully");
} catch (EmptyLineException e) {
    console.printLine("Hello!");
} catch (Exception e) {
    console.printLine("Error: " + e.message());
} finally {
    console.printLine("The program terminates now");
}
```

As a minor variation, some languages use a single handler clause, which deals with the class of the exception internally.

C supports various means of error checking but generally is not considered to support "exception handling." Perl has optional support for structured exception handling.

The C++ derivative Embedded C++ excludes exception handling support as it can substantially increase the size of the object code.

By contrast Python's support for exception handling is pervasive and consistent. It's difficult to write a robust Python program without using its support for ***try:***ing certain operations and catching various ***except:***ions.

Exception handling implementation

The implementation of exception handling typically involves a fair amount of support from both a code generator and the runtime system accompanying a compiler. (It was the addition of exception handling to C++ that ended the useful lifetime of the original C++ compiler, Cfront.) Two schemes are most common. The first, *dynamic registration*, generates code that continually updates structures about the program state in terms of exception handling.[4] Typically, this adds a new element to the stack frame layout that knows what handlers are available for the function or method associated with that frame; if an exception is thrown, a pointer in the layout directs the runtime to the appropriate handler code. This approach is compact in terms of space but adds execution overhead on frame entry and exit. It was commonly used in many Ada implementations, for example, where complex generation and runtime support was already needed for many other language features. Dynamic registration, being fairly straightforward to define, is amenable to proof of correctness.[5]

The second scheme, and the one implemented in many production-quality C++ compilers, is a *table-driven* approach. This creates static tables at compile and link time that relate ranges of the program counter to the program state with respect to exception handling.[6] Then, if an exception is thrown, the runtime system looks up the current instruction location in the tables and determines what handlers are in play and what needs to be done. This approach minimizes executive overhead for the case where an exception is not thrown, albeit at the cost of some space, although said space can be allocated into read-only, special-purpose data sections that are not loaded or relocated until and unless an exception is thrown.[7] This second approach is also superior in terms of achieving thread safety.

Other definitional and implementation schemes have been proposed as well.[8] For languages that support metaprogramming, approaches that involve no overhead at all have been advanced.[9]

Exception handling based on Design by Contract

A different view of exceptions is based on the principles of Design by Contract and is supported in particular by the Eiffel language. The idea is to provide a more rigorous basis for exception handling by defining precisely what is "normal" and "abnormal" behavior. Specifically, the approach is based on two concepts:

- **Failure**: the inability of an operation to fulfill its contract. For example an addition may produce an arithmetic overflow (it does not fulfill its contract of computing a good approximation to the mathematical sum); or a routine may fail to meet its postcondition.
- **Exception**: an abnormal event occurring during the execution of a routine (that routine is the "*recipient*" of the exception) during its execution. Such an abnormal event results from the *failure* of an operation called by the routine.

The "Safe Exception Handling principle" as introduced by Bertrand Meyer in Object-Oriented Software Construction then holds that there are only two meaningful ways a routine can react when an exception occurs:

- Failure, or "organized panic": the routine fails, triggering an exception in its caller (so that the abnormal event is not ignored!), after fixing the object's state by re-establishing the invariant (the "organized" part).
- Retry: try the algorithm again, usually after changing some values so that the next attempt will have a better chance to succeed.

Here is an example expressed in Eiffel syntax. It assumes that a routine *send_fast* is normally the better way to send a message, but it may fail, triggering an exception; if so, the algorithm next uses *send_slow*, which will fail less often. If *send_slow* fails, the routine send as a whole should fail, causing the caller to get an exception.

```
send (m: MESSAGE) is
      -- Send m through fast link if possible, otherwise through slow link.
local
      tried_fast, tried_slow: BOOLEAN
do
      if tried_fast then
         tried_slow := True
         send_slow (m)
      else
         tried_fast := True
         send_fast (m)
      end
rescue
      if not tried_slow then
         retry
      end
end
```

The boolean local variables are initialized to False at the start. If *send_fast* fails, the body (**do** clause) will be executed again, causing execution of *send_slow*. If this execution of *send_slow* fails, the **rescue** clause will execute to the end with no **retry** (no **else** clause in the final **if**), causing the routine execution as a whole to fail.

This approach has the merit of defining clearly what a "normal" and "abnormal" cases are: an abnormal case, causing an exception, is one in which the routine is unable to fulfill its contract.

It defines a clear distribution of roles: the **do** clause (normal body) is in charge of achieving, or attempting to achieve, the routine's contract; the **rescue** clause is in charge of reestablishing the context and restarting the process if this has a chance of succeeding, but not of performing any actual computation.

Checked exceptions

The designers of Java devised[10] [11] checked exceptions,[12] which are a special set of exceptions. The checked exceptions that a method may raise are part of the method's signature. For instance, if a method might throw an IOException, it must declare this fact explicitly in its method signature. Failure to do so raises a compile-time error.

This is related to exception checkers that exist at least for OCaml.[13] The external tool for OCaml is both transparent (i.e. it does not require any syntactic annotations) and facultative (i.e. it is possible to compile and run a program without having checked the exceptions, although this is not suggested for production code).

The CLU programming language had a feature with the interface closer to what Java has introduced later. A function could raise only exceptions listed in its type, but any leaking exceptions from called functions would automatically be turned into the sole runtime exception, failure, instead of resulting in compile-time error. Later, Modula-3 had a similar feature.[14] These features don't include the compile time checking which is central in the concept of checked exceptions, and hasn't (as of 2006) been incorporated into major programming languages other than Java.[15]

The C++ programming language introduces an optional mechanism for checked exceptions, called *exception specifications*. By default any function can throw any exception, but this can be limited by a throw clause added to the function signature, that specifies which exceptions the function may throw. Exception specifications are not enforced at compile-time. Violations result in the global function std::unexpected being called.[16] An empty exception specification may be given, which indicates that the function will throw no exception. This was not made the default when exception handling was added to the language because it would require too much modification of existing code, would impede interaction with code written in another language, and would tempt programmers into writing too many handlers at the local level.[16] Explicit use of empty exception specifications can, however, allow C++ compilers to perform significant code and stack layout optimizations that normally have to be suppressed when exception handling may take place in a function.[7] Some analysts view the proper use of exception specifications in C++ as difficult to achieve.[17] In the upcoming C++ language standard (C++0x), the use of exception specifications as specified in the current version of the standard (C++03), is deprecated.

Views on usage

Checked exceptions can, at compile time, reduce the incidence of unhandled exceptions surfacing at runtime in a given application; the unchecked exceptions (RuntimeExceptions and Errors) remain unhandled.

However, checked exceptions can either require extensive throws declarations, revealing implementation details and reducing encapsulation, or encourage coding poorly-considered try/catch blocks that can hide legitimate exceptions from their appropriate handlers. Consider a growing codebase over time. An interface may be declared to throw exceptions X & Y. In a later version of the code, if one wants to throw exception Z, it would make the new code incompatible with the earlier uses. Furthermore, with the adapter pattern, where one body of code declares an interface that is then implemented by a different body of code so that code can be plugged in and called by the first, the adapter code may have a rich set of exceptions to describe problems, but is forced to use the exception types declared in the interface.

It is possible to reduce the number of declared exceptions by either declaring a superclass of all potentially thrown exceptions or by defining and declaring exception types that are suitable for the level of abstraction of the called method,[18] and mapping lower level exceptions to these types, preferably wrapped using the exception chaining in order to preserve the root cause. In addition, it's very possible that in the example above of the changing interface that the calling code would need to be modified as well, since in some sense the exceptions a method may throw are part of the method's implicit interface anyway.

Using a minimal throws Exception declaration or catch (Exception e) is sufficient for satisfying the checking in Java. While this may have some use, it essentially circumvents the checked exception mechanism, and forces all calling code to catch (Exception e) or add throws Exception to its method signature.

Unchecked exception types should not be handled except, with consideration, at the outermost levels of scope. These often represent scenarios that do not allow for recovery: RuntimeExceptions frequently reflect programming defects,[19] and Errors generally represent unrecoverable JVM failures. The view is that, even in a language that supports checked exceptions, there are cases where the use of checked exceptions is not appropriate.

Exception synchronicity

Somewhat related with the concept of checked exceptions is *exception synchronicity*. Synchronous exceptions happen at a specific program statement whereas **asynchronous exceptions** can raise practically anywhere.[20] [21] It follows that asynchronous exception handling can't be required by the compiler. They are also difficult to program with. Examples of naturally asynchronous events include pressing Ctrl-C to interrupt a program, and receiving a signal such as "stop" or "suspend" from another thread of execution.

Programming languages typically deal with this by limiting asynchronicity, for example Java has lost thread stopping and resuming.[22] Instead, there can be semi-asynchronous exceptions that only raise in suitable locations of the program or synchronously.

Condition systems

Common Lisp, Dylan and Smalltalk have a Condition system [23] (see Common Lisp Condition System) which encompasses the aforementioned exception handling systems. In those languages or environments the advent of a condition (a "generalisation of an error" according to Kent Pitman) implies a function call, and only late in the exception handler the decision to unwind the stack may be taken.

Conditions are a generalization of exceptions. When a condition arises, an appropriate condition handler is searched for and selected, in stack order, to handle the condition. Conditions which do not represent errors may safely go unhandled entirely; their only purpose may be to propagate hints or warnings toward the user.[24]

Continuable exceptions

This is related to the so-called *resumption model* of exception handling, in which some exceptions are said to be *continuable*: it is permitted to return to the expression that signaled an exception, after having taken corrective action in the handler. The condition system is generalized thus: within the handler of a non-serious condition (a.k.a. *continuable exception*), it is possible to jump to predefined restart points (a.k.a. *restarts*) that lie between the signaling expression and the condition handler. Restarts are functions closed over some lexical environment, allowing the programmer to repair this environment before exiting the condition handler completely or unwinding the stack even partially.

Restarts separate mechanism from policy

Condition handling moreover provides a separation of mechanism from policy. Restarts provide various possible mechanisms for recovering from error, but do not select which mechanism is appropriate in a given situation. That is the province of the condition handler, which (since it is located in higher-level code) has access to a broader view.

An example: Suppose there is a library function whose purpose is to parse a single syslog file entry. What should this function do if the entry is malformed? There is no one right answer, because the same library could be deployed in programs for many different purposes. In an interactive log-file browser, the right thing to do might be to return the entry unparsed, so the user can see it—but in an automated log-summarizing program, the right thing to do might be to supply null values for the unreadable fields, but abort with an error if too many entries have been malformed.

That is to say, the question can only be answered in terms of the broader goals of the program, which are not known to the general-purpose library function. Nonetheless, exiting with an error message is only rarely the right answer. So instead of simply exiting with an error, the function may *establish restarts* offering various ways to continue—for instance, to skip the log entry, to supply default or null values for the unreadable fields, to ask the user for the missing values, *or* to unwind the stack and abort processing with an error message. The restarts offered constitute the *mechanisms* available for recovering from error; the selection of restart by the condition handler supplies the *policy*.

See also

- Abrahams guarantees
- Continuation
- setjmp/longjmp
- Triple fault
- Vectored Exception Handling (VEH)

References

[1] All Exceptions Are Handled, Jim Wilcox, http://poliTechnosis.kataire.com/2008/02/all-exceptions-are-handled.html

[2] http://www.open-std.org/jtc1/sc22/wg21/docs/papers/1997/N1077.asc

[3] Bjarne Stroustrup's FAQ (http://www2.research.att.com/~bs/bs_faq2.html#finally)

[4] D. Cameron, P. Faust, D. Lenkov, M. Mehta, "A portable implementation of C++ exception handling", *Proceedings of the C++ Conference* (August 1992) USENIX.

[5] Graham Hutton, Joel Wright, " Compiling Exceptions Correctly (http://www.cs.nott.ac.uk/~gmh/exceptions.pdf)". *Proceedings of the 7th International Conference on Mathematics of Program Construction*, 2004.

[6] Lajoie, Josée (March–April 1994). "Exception handling – Supporting the runtime mechanism". *C++ Report* **6** (3).

[7] Schilling, Jonathan L. (August 1998). "Optimizing away C++ exception handling". *SIGPLAN Notices* **33** (8): 40–47. doi:10.1145/286385.286390.

[8] " How to Implement Software Exception Handling (http://intel.com/cd/ids/developer/asmo-na/eng/81438.htm)", Intel Corporation.

[9] M. Hof, H. Mössenböck, P. Pirkelbauer, " Zero-Overhead Exception Handling Using Metaprogramming (http://www.ssw.uni-linz.ac.at/Research/Papers/Hof97b.html)", *Proceedings SOFSEM'97*, November 1997, *Lecture Notes in Computer Science 1338*, pp. 423-431.

[10] LISTSERV 15.0 - RMI-USERS Archives (http://archives.java.sun.com/cgi-bin/wa?A2=ind9901&L=rmi-users&F=P&P=36083)

[11] Google Answers: The origin of checked exceptions (http://answers.google.com/answers/threadview?id=26101)

[12] Java Language Specification, chapter 11.2. http://java.sun.com/docs/books/jls/third_edition/html/exceptions.html#11.2

[13] OcamlExc -- An uncaught exceptions analyzer for Objective Caml (http://caml.inria.fr/pub/old_caml_site/ocamlexc/ocamlexc.htm)

[14] Modula-3 - Procedure Types (http://www1.cs.columbia.edu/graphics/modula3/tutorial/www/m3_23.html#SEC23)

[15] Bruce Eckel's MindView, Inc: Does Java need Checked Exceptions? (http://www.mindview.net/Etc/Discussions/CheckedExceptions)

[16] Bjarne Stroustrup, *The C++ Programming Language* Third Edition, Addison Wesley, 1997. ISBN 0-201-88954-4. pp. 375-380.

[17] Reeves, J.W. (July 1996). "Ten Guidelines for Exception Specifications". *C++ Report* **8** (7).

[18] Bloch 2001:178 Bloch, Joshua (2001). *Effective Java Programming Language Guide*. Addison-Wesley Professional. ISBN 0-201-31005-8.

[19] Bloch 2001:172

[20] Asynchronous Exceptions in Haskell - Marlow, Jones, Moran (ResearchIndex) (http://citeseer.ist.psu.edu/415348.html)

[21] Safe asynchronous exceptions for Python. http://www.cs.williams.edu/~freund/papers/02-lwl2.ps

[22] Java Thread Primitive Deprecation (http://java.sun.com/j2se/1.5.0/docs/guide/misc/threadPrimitiveDeprecation.html)

[23] What Conditions (Exceptions) are Really About (http://danweinreb.org/blog/what-conditions-exceptions-are-really-about)

[24] Condition System Concepts (http://www.franz.com/support/documentation/6.2/ansicl/section/conditio.htm)

External links

- Article " PHP exception handling (http://www.chrisjhill.co.uk/Articles/PHP_exception_handling)" by Christopher Hill
- Article " Unchecked Exceptions - The Controversy (http://java.sun.com/docs/books/tutorial/essential/exceptions/runtime.html)"
- Article " Practical C++ Error Handling in Hybrid Environments (http://ddj.com/dept/debug/197003350)" by Gigi Sayfan
- Article " C++ Exception Handling (https://db.usenix.org/events/wiess2000/full_papers/dinechin/dinechin.pdf)" by Christophe de Dinechin
- Article " Exceptional practices (http://java.sun.com/developer/technicalArticles/Programming/exceptions2/index.html)" by Brian Goetz
- Article " Programming with Exceptions in C++ (http://oreillynet.com/pub/a/network/2003/05/05/cpluspocketref.html)" by Kyle Loudon
- Article " Object Oriented Exception Handling in Perl (http://perl.com/pub/a/2002/11/14/exception.html)" by Arun Udaya Shankar
- Article " Exception Handling in C without C++ (http://www.on-time.com/ddj0011.htm)" by Tom Schotland and Peter Petersen
- Article " Structured Exception Handling Basics (http://www.gamedev.net/reference/programming/features/sehbasics/)" by Vadim Kokielov
- Article " All Exceptions Are Handled (http://politechnosis.kataire.com/2008/02/all-exceptions-are-handled.html)" by James "Jim" Wilcox

- Article " An Exceptional Philosophy (http://www.dlugosz.com/Magazine/WTJ/May96/)" by John M. Dlugosz
- Paper " Exception Handling in Petri-Net-based Workflow Management (http://www.informatik.uni-hamburg.de/TGI/pnbib/f/faustmann_g1.html)" by Gert Faustmann and Dietmar Wikarski
- Descriptions from Portland Pattern Repository (http://c2.com/cgi/wiki?CategoryException)
- A Crash Course on the Depths of Win32 Structured Exception Handling (http://www.microsoft.com/msj/0197/exception/exception.aspx) by Matt Pietrek - Microsoft Systems Journal (1997)
- The Trouble with Checked Exceptions (http://artima.com/intv/handcuffsP.html) - a conversation with Anders Hejlsberg
- Does Java Need Checked Exceptions? (http://www.mindview.net/Etc/Discussions/CheckedExceptions)
- Problems and Benefits of Exception Handling (http://neil.fraser.name/writing/exception/)
- Understanding and Using Exceptions in .NET (http://codebetter.com/blogs/karlseguin/archive/2006/04/05/142355.aspx)
- Java Exception Handling (http://tutorials.jenkov.com/java-exception-handling/index.html) - Jakob Jenkov
- Visual Prolog Exception Handling (http://wiki.visual-prolog.com/index.php?title=Exception_Handling) (wiki article)
- Type of Java Exceptions (http://javapapers.com/core-java/java-exception/explain-type-of-exceptions-or-checked-vs-unchecked-exceptions-in-java/)
- Java : How to rethrow exceptions without wrapping them. (http://robaustin.wikidot.com/rethrow-exceptions) - Rob Austin
- How to handle class constructors that fail (http://www.amcgowan.ca/blog/computer-science/how-to-handle-class-constructors-that-fail/)

Fail soft

Fail-soft operation is a characteristic of computing that refers to the ability of a system to fail in such a way as to preserve as much capability and data as possible.[1]

See also

Graceful degradation

References

[1] Stallings, W (2009): Operating Systems. Internals and Design Principles, *sixth edition*

Fault (technology)

In document ISO/CD 10303-226, a **fault** is defined as an abnormal condition or defect at the component, equipment, or sub-system level which may lead to a failure.

According to the Federal Standard 1037C of the United States, the term *fault* has the following meanings:

1. An accidental condition that causes a functional unit to fail to perform its required function.
2. A defect that causes a reproducible or catastrophic malfunction. A malfunction is considered reproducible if it occurs consistently under the same circumstances.
3. In power systems, an unintentional short-circuit, or partial short-circuit, between energized conductors or between an energized conductor and ground. A distinction can be made between symmetric and asymmetric faults.

Failures in hardware can be caused by random faults or systematic faults, but failures in software are always systematic.

See also

- Computer bug
- Defect
- Anomaly in software

Fragile binary interface problem

The **fragile binary interface problem** or **FBI** is a shortcoming of certain object-oriented programming language compilers, in which internal changes to an underlying class library can cause descendant libraries or programs to cease working. It is an example of software brittleness.

Note that this problem is more often called the **fragile base class problem** or **FBC**; however, that term also has a different (but related) sense. (*See* fragile base class.)

Cause

The problem occurs due to a "shortcut" used with compilers for many common object-oriented (OO) languages, a design feature that was kept when OO languages were evolving from earlier non-OO structured programming languages such as C and Pascal.

In these languages there were no objects in the modern sense, but there was a similar construct known as a record (or "struct" in C) that held a variety of related information in one piece of memory. The parts within a particular record were accessed by keeping track of the starting location of the record, and knowing the offset from that starting point to the part in question. For instance a "person" record might have a first name, last name and middle initial, to access the initial the programmer writes thisPerson.middleInitial which the compiler turns into something like a = location(thisPerson) + offset(middleInitial). Modern CPUs typically include instructions for this common sort of access.

When object-oriented language compilers were first being developed, much of the existing compiler technology was used, and objects were built on top of the record concept. In these languages the objects were referred to by their starting point, and their public data, known as "fields", were accessed through the known offset. In effect the only change was to add another field to the record, one that lists the various methods (functions), such that the record knows about both its data and functions. When compiled, the offsets are used to access both the data and the code.

Symptoms

This leads to a problem in larger programs when they are constructed from libraries. If the author of the library changes the size or layout of the public fields within the object, the offsets are now invalid and the program will no longer work. This is the FBI problem.

Although changes in implementation may be expected to cause problems, the insidious thing about FBI is that nothing *really* changed, only the layout of the object that is hidden in a compiled library. One might expect that if you change doSomething to doSomethingElse that it might cause a problem, but in this case you can cause problems without changing doSomething, it can be caused as easily as moving lines of source code around for clarity. Worse, the programmer has little or no control over the resulting layout generated by the compiler, making this problem almost completely hidden from view.

In complex object-oriented programs or libraries the highest-level classes may be inheriting from tens of classes. Each of those base classes could be inherited by hundreds of other classes as well. These base classes are fragile because a small change to one of them could cause problems for any class that inherits from it, either directly or from inheriting another class that does. This can cause the library to collapse like a house of cards as many classes are damaged by one change to a base class. The problem may not be noticed as the modifications are being written if the inheritance tree is complex.

Solutions

Languages

The best solution to the fragile binary interface problem is to write a language that knows the problem exists, and does not let it happen in the first place. Most custom-written OO languages, as opposed to those evolved from earlier languages, construct all of their offset tables at load time. Changes to the layout of the library will be "noticed" at that point. Other OO languages, like Self, construct everything at runtime by copying and modifying the objects found in the libraries, and therefore do not really have a base class that can be fragile. Some languages, like Java, have extensive documentation on what changes are safe to make without causing FBI problems.

Another solution is to write out an intermediate file listing the offsets and other information from the compile stage, known as meta-data. The linker then uses this information to correct itself when the library is loaded into an application. Platforms such as .NET do this.

However, the market has selected programming languages such as C++ that are indeed "position dependent" and therefore exhibit FBI. In these cases there are still a number of solutions to the problem. One puts the burden on the library author by having them insert a number of "placeholder" objects in case they need to add additional functionality in the future (this can be seen in the structs used in the DirectX library). This solution works well until you run out of these dummies -- and you do not want to add too many because it takes up memory.

Linkers

Another solution requires a smarter linker. In Objective-C, the library format allowed for multiple versions of one library and included some functionality for selecting the proper library when called. However this was not always needed because the offsets were only needed for fields, since methods offsets were collected at runtime and could not cause FBI. Since methods tend to change more often than fields, ObjC had few FBI problems in the first place, and those it did could be corrected with the versioning system. The TOM language has extended this even further, using runtime collected offsets for everything, making FBI impossible.

Using static instead of dynamic libraries where possible is another solution, as the library then cannot be modified without also recompiling the application and updating the offsets it uses. However static libraries have serious problems of their own, such as a larger binary and the inability to use newer versions of the library "automatically" as they are introduced.

The vast majority of programming languages in use today do nothing to protect the programmer from FBI. This is somewhat surprising, as the problem has been known about since the 1980s.

Architecture

In these languages the problem is lessened by enforcing single inheritance (as this reduces the complexity of the inheritance tree), and by the use of interfaces instead of base classes with virtual functions, as interfaces themselves do not contain code, only a guarantee that each method signature the interface declares will be supported by every object that implements the interface.

Distribution method

The whole problem collapses if the source code of the used libraries is available. Then a simple recompilation will do the trick.

See also

- Fragile base class

External links

- BeOS's paper [1] on the problem and their solution

References

[1] http://2f.ru/holy-wars/fbc.html

Glitch

A **glitch** is a short-lived fault in a system. It is often used to describe a transient fault that corrects itself, and is therefore difficult to troubleshoot. The term is particularly common in the computing and electronics industries, and in circuit bending, as well as among players of video games, although it is applied to all types of systems including human organizations and nature.

The term derives from the German *glitschig,* meaning 'slippery', possibly entering English through the Yiddish term *glitsh*.

Electronics glitch

An **electronics glitch** is an undesired transition that occurs before the signal settles to its intended value. In other words, glitch is an electrical pulse of short duration that is usually the result of a fault or design error, particularly in a digital circuit. For example, many electronic components such as flip-flops are triggered by a pulse that must not be shorter than a specified minimum duration, otherwise the component may malfunction. A pulse shorter than the specified minimum is called a glitch. A related concept is the runt pulse, a pulse whose amplitude is smaller than the minimum level specified for correct operation, and a spike, a short pulse similar to a glitch but often caused by ringing or crosstalk. A *glitch* can occur in the presence of race condition in a poorly designed digital logic circuit.

Computer glitch

A **computer glitch** is the failure of a system, usually containing a computing device, to complete its functions or to perform them properly. In public declarations, glitch is used to suggest a minor fault which will soon be rectified and is therefore a euphemism by comparison to bug, which is a factual statement that a programming fault is to blame for a system failure.

It frequently refers to an error which is not detected at the time it occurs but shows up later in data errors or incorrect human decisions. While the fault is usually attributed to the computer hardware, this is often not the case since hardware failures rarely go undetected. Situations which are frequently called computer glitches are:

- Incorrectly written software (software bug)
- Incorrect instructions given by the operator (operator error) (this might also be considered a software bug)
- Undetected invalid input data (this might also be considered a software bug)
- Undetected communications errors
- Computer viruses
- Computer security cracking (sometimes erroneously called "hacking")
- Another human error unrelated to the computer

An example of a computer glitch was in 2008 that brought down the primary patient application to 17 United States Department of Veterans Affairs medical centers in Northern California. The cause was from a simple change in management procedure that was not properly followed.[1]

Etymology

Canadian Oxford lists it as a 20th century word of unknown origin. Some reference books, including *Random House's American Slang*, it comes from the German word *glitschen* ("to slip") and the Yiddish word *gletshn* ("to slide or skid"). Either way it is a relatively new term. So new, in fact, that on July 23, 1965, *Time Magazine* felt it necessary to define it in an article: "Glitches—a spaceman's word for irritating disturbances."

Video game glitches

In video games, a glitch is a programming error which results in behavior not intended by the programmers. Glitches may include incorrectly displayed graphics, collision detection errors, game freezes/crashes, sound issues, and others. Some glitches are potentially dangerous to the game save data.[2]

"Glitching" is the practice of a player exploiting faults in a video game's programming to achieve tasks normally impossible if the game's script runs as intended, such as running through walls or defying the game's laws of gravity. It is often used to gain an unfair advantage over other players in multiplayer video games.

During quality assurance (such as the role of a game tester for video games), glitches must be located, a report compiled, and then fed back to the programmers.[2]

Most of these glitches are used in campaign/story mode, and for online multi-player in games like Call of Duty: Modern Warfare 2, Black Ops, Halo 3, Halo Reach, and thousands of other online games for Xbox 360, Playstation 3, and the Wii. People can find these glitches at websites that provide glitches, such as GamerGlitches [3]. You can then see the video tutorial of how to perform the glitch there.

Popular culture

- In the 1987 science fiction film *RoboCop* directed by Paul Verhoeven, ED-209, a state-of-the-art military robot, malfunctions during its presentation to the executive board of the fictional OCP (Omni Consumer Products). The result is the brutal killing of a company executive. Shortly after the incident, another executive states that it happened due to a "minor glitch".
- In the 1999 film *The Matrix* there's a "glitch in the Matrix", a sense of déjà vu that occurs when the enemy machines alter an aspect of the Matrix, a digital reality in which all the inhabitants believe that they are living in the real world. This is seen when the protagonist, Neo, sees a black cat walk by twice.
- In the 1994-2001 computer animated series ReBoot the character of Bob has a key tool called "Glitch". This is a reference to a computer glitch.

A 1976 novel by Steve Wilson, *The Lost Traveller*, deals with a post-apocalyptic world in which descendants of the Hell's Angels motorcycle gang act as paramilitary forces for a community called the Fief. Over the years, the Angels have developed numerous quasi-religious beliefs, including a pantheon of gods. One of the minor deities is Glitch, the godlet of hangups and, well, glitches.


```
Most of these glitches are used in campaign/story mode, and for online
multi-player in games like Call of Duty: Modern Warfare 2, Black Ops,
Halo 3, Halo Reach, and thousands of other online games for Xbox 360,
Playstation 3, and the Wii.
```

See also

- Glitch (music)
- Hazard
- Boot
- Anomaly in software
- Glitching
- Glitch Art
- Software bug
- Cartridge tilting

References

[1] Maddox, Michael. "Infamous computer glitch". *Industrial Engineer*. p. 20. Article also mentions definition of computer glitch in Wikipedia.
[2] Ofoe, Emmanuel-Yvan; William Pare (March 06 - March 12.2008). "Testing, testing, testing" (http://www.montrealmirror.com/2008/030608/games1.html). Montreal Mirror. . Retrieved 2008-06-17.
[3] http://gamerglitches.com

Glitch art

Glitch art is the aestheticization of digital or analog errors, such as artifacts and other "bugs", by either corrupting digital code/data or by physically manipulating electronic devices (for example by circuit bending).

Glitch

In a technical sense a glitch is the unexpected result of a malfunction. The term is thought to derive from the German *glitschig*, meaning 'slippery.' It was first recorded in English in 1962 during the American space program by John Glenn when describing problems they were having, Glenn explained, "Literally, a glitch is a spike or change in voltage in an electrical current."[1]

Glitch is used to describe these kinds of bugs as they occur in software, video games, images, videos, audio, and other forms of data. The term glitch came to be associated with music in the mid 90s to describe a genre of experimental/noise/electronica (see Glitch (music). Shortly after, as VJs and other visual artist like Tony (Ant) Scott began to embrace the glitch as an aesthetic of the digital age, glitch art came to refer to a whole assembly of visual arts.

In January 2002, Motherboard, a tech-art collective held a glitch symposium in Oslo, Norway, to "bring together international artists, academics and other Glitch practitioners for a short space of time to share their work and ideas with the public and with each other."[2]

Iman Moradi, perhaps the first official glitch theorist, has written extensively on the subject of glitch art and released the book *Glitch: Designing Imperfections* in September 2009.

Glitch as art

Glitches are mostly a result of miscommunication or mistranslation when transferring data from one environment to another. They occur in computers due to bugs in software or hardware. In Iman Moradi's dissertation, *Glitch Aesthetics*, he divides the glitch into two categories. The first is the pure glitch which is the result of a Malfunction or Error, an unpremeditated digital artifact, which may or may not have its own aesthetic merits. The second is the glitch-alike which is the result of an intentional decision on the user side. Glitch artists either synthesize glitches in non-digital mediums, or produce and create the environment that is required to invoke a glitch and anticipate one. A glitch-alike then is a collection of digital artifacts that resemble visual aspects of real glitches found in their original habitat.[1]

In his dissertation Moradi lists some common glitch characteristics: fragmentation (shifted parts or elements of the original image as well as tonal changes), replication/repetition (the visual cloning or repetition of any given part of an image), linearity (as a result of digital's interlacing and pixel structures), complexity, (manifestation of the immense series of code beneath any piece of digital media).

Whether naturally occurring (pure glitch) or instigated (glitch-alike) there are numerous situations that may result in glitches. They can occur as a result of a scratched DVD, a corrupted stream of video on the internet or digital television, a software crash due to insufficient memory, a malfunctioning digital camera or other device. These glitches sometimes cause garbled patterns to appear on the screen. In these ways, it is argued, the glitch can be viewed as a found object similar to the ready-made. An artist/user/hacker can also cause these situations to happen deliberately; e.g., he/she can corrupt the code of a particular digital file or even physically manipulate (intentionally malfunction) the circuits of a digital device, forcing it to glitch its output, in the same way a circuit bender could with a child's toy to create unique sounds (see circuit bending). After the occurrence of a glitch (whether or not resulting from intention) it can be presented purely, as a corrupt file to be interpreted by a computer or other digital device. Glitches can also be manipulated (e.g., colors can be changed [as in Tony (Ant) Scott's work], clips can be edited) and then saved as stable files. These files can then be printed or burned to a DVD or other media. "The glitch aesthetic seeks to select regions of interest from this often very rich raw material input, digitally manipulate it, and produce images which are pleasing to the artist." [3]

> The genre of the glitch and its role in a conceptual framework can be considered as an art form. In its visual and practical manifestations though, glitches and glitch-alikes have a distinct medium like quality. They exist within other media but their often out of place characteristics have the capacity to convey a message and that is what makes them an effective medium, sub-medium or accompanying medium. The Glitch imagery may be unrecognizable from its source data, but the source is usually implied or can be perceived in an obvious manner in order for the glitch process to fulfill its objective existence, in particular when it comes to conveying meaning. The creation of Glitch-alike artwork doesn't have to result in the conveyance of meaning, it can be fulfilling and satisfying as a process in itself. ... In the world of perfect telecommunication, glitches are undesirables for which countless error checking protocols exist with the sole purpose of eliminating them. In terms of representation, the ones that don't make it into modes of audio or visual communication are merely represented as a trace log of error occurrences that could be used to eliminate further instances before they happen. This symptomatic lack of function or unwanted function in society, gives the glitch its unique status in art.[1]

Glitch history, context, and appreciation

> As a signifier of data, glitch art is often so obtuse that most casual viewers would not have the technical savvy to fully understand the processes and sources of the information they are seeing. Thus, the viewer's experience with a glitch art piece involves a personal awareness of computing and technology. Some of the work requires just menial technological experience -- any child of the 80's would recognize the familiar blips and digital warps that might arise from an incorrectly-loaded Nintendo cartridge. But the aesthetic and conceptual beauty of a visualized Unix core dump (a copy of the contents of memory used by a computing process) is thrown to those who would understand it.[4]

Many comparisons can be made between the glitch's formal aesthetics and those of the art that preceded it. At first glance, the work's blocky, low-res aesthetics appear formally reminiscent of the most geometric of modernist abstract art, particularly the rectangular forms of de Stijl works like Mondrian's earlier Composition pieces and some Bauhaus or Expressionist works of Klee, Rothko, and Kandinsky. These artists avoided direct visual representations of figurative reality, in favor of experiments in spontaneity, absolutes, or studies in form, color, or shape.[4] Another similar connection can be made to the cubist works of Picasso and Braque. The incorporation of chance operations/experiments by John Cage and others in their work is a philosophy shared by many glitch artists who manipulate digital files and devices sometimes at random in anticipation of the results. This tendency to experiment with the physical medium is also very similar to the approach taken by many avant-garde filmmakers like Stan Brakhage who would paint, scratch, and manipulate in countless ways the actual celluloid addressing the medium by exploiting its imperfections. A history for appreciation of imperfections can also be seen in the works of artist like Gerhard Richter, who recreates the flaws found in photographs in his paintings, as well as in Mondrian's work which, though seemingly perfect, is marked by varying elements which disrupt this perfection. These connections to more traditional artistic mediums may account for glitch's appreciation today.

> Today's trend of 'perfection' in communication reminds us less of our past when communications were 'imperfect' and anything that glitches brings us closer to experiencing that past. This is partly why glitches are sometimes coupled with retro aesthetics, and it may be part of the reason for their appreciation. Glitch artists who were children of the eighties and nineties may comment on this especially.[1]

Glitch artists

In contrast to the digital artists who aim to produce hyper-realistic images (e.g., Jurassic Park, through the use of high-end 3-D computer graphics, the glitch artist uses the computer as a tool for exploring the digital medium and its inherent aesthetic potential, as well as a tool for manipulating it. "The glitch artist assumes a role akin to that of a photographer, exploring the environment, waiting for interesting events to happen, and capturing the image before it disappears."[3] For these artists, glitch art is process that stems from an understanding of their tools: computer hardware, software, display adapters, storage media, etc.[1]

> Glitching is a process of creating work that raises awareness of the means by which we communicate and ultimately exteriorize thought. It is an attempt to integrate the nebula of video with a concrete process of interpretation and injunction, thereby incorporating the properties of a medium into the narrative of its content. At very least, glitch-art functions as a reminder that the technology of digital production and information theory remains as an inexorable collaborator in all works of digital propagation and therefore should be treated as significant.[5]

Glitches and popular culture

Though glitching may often involve a complicated systemized process of file corruption or hardware manipulation there are also very simple and commonly known methods for glitching such as the "word pad glitch." This is as simple as opening an uncompressed image file (bmp, tif) in Microsoft WordPad and clicking save. When you open the file as an image again after having saved it on WordPad the result is a glitched version of the original.[6]

Datamoshing

One form of glitching which has recently become very popular is called "Datamoshing." **Datamoshing** occurs when the I-frames or key-frames of a temporally compressed video are removed, causing frames from different video sequences to bleed together. The popularity of datamoshing can be attributed to the creator of a Chairlift music video and his on-line tutorials on his particular method.[7]

Spread

These kinds of tutorials as well as interactive works like the glitch browser (by Lima, Moradi and Scott) and Corrupt (by Benjamin Gaulon) in addition to online groups/communities like the Flickr Glitch Art group have all been contributing factors to the democratization of glitch as a digital art form. There are also devices (hardware) that have been known to have common glitches. The iPhone for example has a very particular glitch that occurs often when taking pictures.[8] [9]

Commercialization

The use of the glitch aesthetic has recently begun to appear in commercial media such as advertising/television commercials (e.g., Absolut Vodka), Hollywood films (e.g., Cloverfield), and music videos such as the Kanye West video "Welcome to Heartbreak." This particular use of the glitch has been met with some criticism. Angela Lorenz, suggests in the case of the visual glitch, marketing executives are exploiting styles they see without considering or promoting any experimentation, according to Lorenz, they "try to make themselves appear more interesting / appealing to a 'young' audience by hopping onto a certain 'trend'".[1]

Aesthetics

The aesthetics of the glitch have also recently been mimicked and re-created by other means (using traditional design tools/software) and used in a more traditional art sense. Artists and designers like metaphsk and ratsi have all adopted the glitch's look and begun to apply it to their work. There exist web tutorials that explain how to re-create the glitch aesthetic using programs like Jitter.[10] It is important to note that there is a distinction between a work which is actually corrupted (where there occurs a kind of collaboration between the computer and the glitch practitioner) and a work which adopts some of the glitch's characteristics and achieves similar results by secondary means.

See also

- Circuit bending
- Datamoshing
- Glitch
- Glitch (music)
- Glitching
- New media art

References

[1] Moradi, Iman. (2004) Glitch Aesthetic http://www.oculasm.org/glitch/download/Glitch_dissertation_print_with_pics.pdf
[2] Motherboard. (2002) http://www.liveart.org/motherboard/
[3] Scott, Tony. (2002) Glitch on Paper http://beflix.com/gop.html
[4] Downey, Jonas. Glitch Art http://half-a-world-away.com/about
[5] Meaney, Evan. (2008) on glitching http://www.evanmeaney.com/glitching/theory/evan_meaney_onglitching.pdf
[6] WordPad Glitch tutorial (http://www.animalswithinanimals.com/stallio/2008/08/databending-and-glitch-art-primer-part.html)
[7] Chairlift video (http://www.youtube.com/watch?v=tYytVzbPky8)
[8] iPhone Cubism (http://flickr.com/groups/iphonecubism/)
[9] iPhone Camera Art (http://flickr.com/groups/iphonecameraart/)
[10] Jitter (http://abstrakt.vade.info/?p=48)

Glitching

A glitch on *Call of Duty 3*, where the player is below the playing area, looking up.

Glitching is a form of cheating in which a person finds and exploits flaws or glitches in video games to achieve something that was not intended by the game designers. Gamers who engage in this practice are known as glitchers. Glitches can help or disable the player.

"Glitching" is also used to describe the state of a video game undergoing a glitch. The frequency in which a game undergoes glitching is often used by reviewers when examining the overall gameplay,[1] or specific game aspects such as graphics.[2] Some Games such as Metroid have lower review scores today because in retrospect, the game may be very prone to glitches and be below what would be acceptable today.

Video game glitches that go to "out of bounds" areas are mostly performed by either moving through walls or corners or jumping to places in the map that don't have invisible walls. For example, in Tony Hawks Underground 2, in the Los Angeles level there is a glitch that can allow players to leave the proper play area and enter the background and in Half Life 2.

In "out of bounds" areas, many maps have hollow objects that the player can move through freely. These objects usually are in the distance and are for decoration. The floor or terrain can also be hollow. The floor can appear the same as a normal floor but moving over it will cause the player to fall as if it doesn't exist. Depending on the game, after falling a certain distance the player will freeze, die, respawn on the map again or just keep falling. A good example is in the Nintendo 64 game The Legend of Zelda: Ocarina of Time there is a section of "wall" at the entrance to the water temple that will allow players to fall through the ground. Eventually players respawn rather than the game crashing.

The early games of the Pokémon series are famous for their glitches. Players often use the glitches to obtain higher levels for their Pokémon, a large number of items, or multiple Legendary Pokémon. Glitching in *Pokémon* started for the most part with the discovery of MissingNo.. Some other games with glitches are GTA, Tony Hawk Underground on Gamecube and others.

References

[1] ethikal1 (February 8, 2005). "ESPN College Hoops 2K5 Review" (http://rr.ps2.ign.com/rrview/ps2/espn_college_hoops_2k5/683882/23375/). IGN. . Retrieved 2008-06-29. "Fun, until it started glitching"

[2] IGN Staff (March 13, 1998). "Tekken 3 vs. The Rest" (http://uk.psx.ign.com/articles/064/064422p1.html). IGN. . Retrieved 2008-06-29. "GRAPHICS, Bloody Roar: Solid graphics, little glitching"

Handle leak

A **handle leak** is a type of software bug that occurs when a computer program asks for a handle to a resource but does not free the handle when it is no longer used. If this occurs frequently or repeatedly over an extended period of time, a large number of handles may be marked in-use and thus unavailable, causing performance problems or a crash.

The term is derived from memory leak. Handle leaks, like memory leaks, are specific instances of resource leaks.

Causes

One cause of a handle leak is when a programmer mistakenly believes that retrieving a handle to an entity is simply obtaining an unmanaged reference, without understanding that a count, a copy, or other operation may actually be being performed.

An example of this might be retrieving a handle to the display device. Programmers might use this handle to check some property (e.g. querying the supported resolutions), and then simply proceed on without ever releasing the handle. If the handle was just a pointer to some data structure with no additional management, then allowing the handle to pass out of scope would not cause an issue. However, in many cases, such handles must be explicitly closed or released to avoid leaking resources associated with them; the exact requirements for what must be done with a handle varies by interface.

Hang (computing)

In computing, a **hang** or **freeze** occurs when either a single computer program or the whole system ceases to respond to inputs. In the most commonly encountered scenario, a workstation with a graphical user interface, all windows belonging to the frozen program become static, and though the mouse cursor still moves on the screen, neither typing on the keyboard nor clicking the mouse produces any effect in the program's windows. The mouse cursor may also be stuck in a form indicating that it is waiting for some operation to complete, such as an hourglass or a spinning wait cursor. Many modern operating systems provide the user with a means to terminate a hung program without rebooting or logging out. In more severe hangs affecting the whole system, no window belonging to any program will respond to keyboard or mouse input, and often the mouse cursor will freeze in place on the screen. Almost always, the only way to recover from a system freeze is to reboot the machine, usually by power cycling with an on/off or reset button.

A hang differs from a crash, in which a program exits abnormally or the operating system shuts down.

Hangs are not limited to client personal computers with a graphical user interface, as in the example above. Servers can hang as well. In those cases, the server ceases to respond to requests. These sorts of hangs are typically addressed by a solution far more complex than an on/off or reset button.

Pre-emptive multitasking operating systems, such as Microsoft Windows 2000/XP/Vista/7, Apple Computer's Mac OS X and Linux hang less often as the multi-tasking system is not affected by non-terminating loops and further does not require tasks to yield control to the operating system. If a task does hang, the scheduler may switch to another group of interdependent tasks so that all processes will not hang.[1]

Causes

Hardware can cause a computer to hang, either because it is intermittent or because it is mismatched with other hardware in the computer[2] (this can occur when one makes an upgrade). Hardware can also become defective over time due to dirt or heat damage.

A hang can also occur due to the fact that the programmer has incorrect termination conditions for a loop, or, in a co-operative multitasking operating system, forgetting to yield to other tasks. Said differently, many software-related hangs are caused by threads waiting for an event to occur which will never occur.[3] This is also known as an infinite loop.

Another cause of hangs is a race condition in communication between processes. One process may send a signal to a second process then stop execution until it receives a response. If the second process is busy the signal will be forced to wait until the process can get to it. However, if the second process was busy sending a signal to the first process then both processes would wait forever for the other to respond to signals and never see the other's signal (this event is known as a deadlock). If the processes are uninterruptible they will hang and have to be shut down. If at least one of the processes is a critical kernel process the whole system may hang and have to be restarted.

A computer may seem to hang when in fact it is simply processing very slowly. This can be caused by too many programs running at once, not enough memory (RAM), or memory fragmentation, slow hardware access (especially to remote devices), slow system APIs, etc. It can also be caused by hidden programs which were installed surreptitiously, such as spyware.

Solutions

In many cases programs may appear to be hung, but are making slow progress, and waiting a few minutes will allow the task to complete.

Usually, in systems with a modern operating system, the user is able to terminate the programs running (for instance, with the kill command, or through the "end task" button on the task list in recent versions of Microsoft Windows), and, if they wish, restart it in the hope that the anomalous condition that caused the hang does not recur. Older systems, such as those using MS-DOS or Windows 3.1x, often needed to be completely restarted in the event of a hang.

A watchdog timer can reboot the computer in the event of a hang (this is commonly used in embedded devices).

References

[1] US 6052707 (http://v3.espacenet.com/textdoc?DB=EPODOC&IDX=US6052707), D'Souza, David, "Preemptive multi-tasking with cooperative groups of tasks", published 1996-06-21, issued 2000-04-18

[2] Microsoft Help and Support (2007-01-27). "How to Troubleshoot Computer Hangs During Hardware Detection" (http://support.microsoft.com/kb/262381). Press release. . Retrieved 2008-07-31.

[3] Calvin Hsia (2006-11-16). *"Here's an infinite loop that will hang your machine"*. [news:blogs.msdn.com blogs.msdn.com]. (Web link) (http://www.feedsfarm.com/article/8738c4141d9874d6e05f6a3e57369280014c7081.html). Retrieved on 2008-07-31.

See also

- Abort (computing)
- Anomaly in software
- Blue screen of death
- Crash (computing)
- Deadlock
- Livelock
- Infinite loop

- Uninterruptible sleep

Heap overflow

A **heap overflow** is a type of buffer overflow that occurs in the heap data area. Heap overflows are exploitable in a different manner to that of stack-based overflows. Memory on the heap is dynamically allocated by the application at run-time and typically contains program data. Exploitation is performed by corrupting this data in specific ways to cause the application to overwrite internal structures such as linked list pointers. The canonical heap overflow technique overwrites dynamic memory allocation linkage (such as malloc meta data) and uses the resulting pointer exchange to overwrite a program function pointer.

Consequences

An accidental overflow may result in data corruption or unexpected behavior by any process which uses the affected memory area. On operating systems without memory protection, this could be any process on the system.

A deliberate exploit may result in data at a specific location being altered in an arbitrary way, or in arbitrary code being executed.

The Microsoft JPEG GDI+ vulnerability MS04-028 [1] is an example of the danger a heap overflow can represent to a computer user.

The iPhone 3Gs and the PS3 have both been exploited by heap overflows to allow homebrew.

Detection and Prevention

Since version 2.3.6 the GNU libc includes protections that can detect heap overflows after the fact, for example by checking pointer consistency when calling *unlink*. While those protections protect against old-style exploits, they are not perfect, as described in The Malloc Maleficarum [2], further described in Malloc Des-Maleficarum [3].

Microsoft Windows operating systems implement protections against heap overflows since Windows XP SP2 such as safe unlinking and cookies. It also can mitigate these threats through the use of Data Execution Prevention (DEP) and ASLR.

Other allocator such as the DieHard [4] allocator can be used to protected against heap overflows and reduces the likelihood of them having any effect on a running program.

External links

- "w00w00 on Heap Overflows", a more detailed explanation of heap overflows [5]
- http://doc.bughunter.net/buffer-overflow/heap-corruption.html [6]
- Heap Overflow article at Heise Security [7]
- Defeating Microsoft Windows XP SP2 Heap protection and DEP bypass [8]

See also

- Buffer overflow
- Stack overflow
- Stack buffer overflow
- Exploit
- Shellcode

References

[1] http://www.microsoft.com/technet/security/bulletin/MS04-028.mspx
[2] http://www.packetstormsecurity.org/papers/attack/MallocMaleficarum.txt
[3] http://www.phrack.org/issues.html?issue=66&id=10#article
[4] http://www.diehard-software.org
[5] http://www.w00w00.org/files/articles/heaptut.txt
[6] http://doc.bughunter.net/buffer-overflow/heap-corruption.html
[7] http://www.heise-online.co.uk/security/A-Heap-of-Risk--/features/74634
[8] http://www.ptsecurity.com/download/defeating-xpsp2-heap-protection.pdf

Interrupt storm

In operating systems, an **interrupt storm** is an event during which a processor receives an inordinate number of interrupts that consume the majority of the processor's time. Interrupt storms are typically caused by hardware devices that do not support interrupt rate limiting.

Background

Because interrupt processing is typically a non-preemptible task in time-sharing operating systems, an interrupt storm will cause low perceived system responsiveness, or even appear to be a complete system freeze. This state is commonly known as *live lock*. In such a state, the system is spending so much time processing interrupts that it is not completing any other work. Therefore, it does not appear to be processing anything at all, because of a lack of output to the user, the network, or otherwise. An interrupt storm is sometimes mistaken for thrashing, since they both have similar symptoms, but different causes.

An interrupt storm can have many different causes, including misconfigured or faulty hardware devices, faulty device drivers, or flaws in the operating system. Most modern hardware implement methods for reducing or eliminating the possibility of an interrupt storm. For example, many Ethernet controllers implement interrupt "rate limiting", which causes the controller to wait a programmable minimum amount of time between each interrupt it generates.

The most common interrupt storm is a faulty driver under an APIC (Advanced Programmable Interrupt Controller) where a device "behind" another signals an interrupt to the APIC. The OS then asks each driver on that interrupt if it was from its hardware. Faulty drivers may always claim "yes", but then proceed no further as the hardware attached actually did not interrupt. The device which originally interrupted did not get its interrupt serviced, so interrupts again and the cycle begins anew. Many operating systems, e.g. Linux, lock dead under an interrupt storm; others have mechanisms to avoid it. This was (and remains) a problem on the SoundBlaster Live! series of sound cards on some motherboards; only a kernel debugger can break the storm by unloading the faulty driver.

Many OSes implement a polling mode that disables interrupts for devices which generate too many interrupts. In this mode, the OS periodically queries the hardware for pending tasks. As the number of interrupts increase and the efficiency of an interrupt mode diminishes, an OS may change the interrupting device from an interrupt mode to a polling mode. Likewise, as the polling mode becomes less efficient than the interrupt mode, the OS will switch the device back to the interrupt mode. The implementation of interrupt rate limiting in hardware almost negates the need for such polling modes.

History

Perhaps the first interrupt storm occurred during the Apollo 11's lunar descent in 1969.

Considerations

Interrupt rate limiting must be carefully configured for optimum results. For example, an Ethernet controller with interrupt rate limiting will buffer the packets it receives from the network in between each interrupt. If the rate is set too high, the controller's buffer will overflow, and packets will be dropped. The rate must take into account how fast the buffer may fill between interrupts, and the interrupt latency between the interrupt and the transfer of the buffer to the system.

Interrupt mitigating

There are hardware-based and software-based approaches to the problem. FreeBSD detects interrupt storms and masks problematic interrupt for some time. Other possible scheme is the one used by NAPI

- System (driver) starts in interrupt enabled state
- Interrupt handler disables the interrupt and lets a thread/task handle the event(s) (example of event is an incoming Ethernet packet)
- Task polls the device, processes some number of events and enables the interrupt

Another interesting approach using hardware support — device generates interrupt when event queue state changes from "empty" to "not empty"

Device

- If there is no free DMA descriptors at the RX FIFO tail drop the event
- Add event to the tail and mark the FIFO entry as occupied
- If entry (tail−1) is free (cleared), generate interrupt (level interrupt)
- Increment tail pointer

CPU (interrupt handler)

- Acknowledge the interrupt (if hardware requires acknowledge)
- Handle all (part of) valid DMA descriptors at head
- return from interrupt

See also

- Broadcast radiation
- Inter-processor interrupt (IPI)
- Non-maskable interrupt (NMI)
- Programmable Interrupt Controller (PIC)

Memory leak

A **memory leak**, in computer science (or **leakage**, in this context), occurs when a computer program consumes memory but is unable to release it back to the operating system. A memory leak has symptoms similar to a number of other problems (see below) and generally can only be diagnosed by a programmer with access to the program source code; however, many people refer to *any* unwanted increase in memory usage as a memory leak, though this is not strictly accurate.

Consequences

A memory leak can diminish the performance of the computer by reducing the amount of available memory. Eventually, in the worst case, too much of the available memory may become allocated and all or part of the system or device stops working correctly, the application fails, or the system slows down unacceptably due to thrashing.

Memory leaks may not be serious or even detectable by normal means. In modern operating systems, normal memory used by an application is released when the application terminates. This means that a memory leak in a program that only runs for a short time may not be noticed and is rarely serious.

Leaks that are much more serious include:

- where the program runs for an extended time and consumes additional memory over time, such as background tasks on servers, but especially in embedded devices which may be left running for many years.
- where new memory is allocated frequently, such as when rendering the frames of a computer game or animated video.
- where the program is able to request memory — such as shared memory — that is not released, even when the program terminates.
- where the leak occurs within the operating system.
- where the leak is the responsibility of a system device driver.
- where memory is very limited, such as in an embedded system or portable device.
- where running on operating systems where memory may not be automatically released on termination, and if lost can only be reclaimed by a reboot (such as AmigaOS).

An example of memory leak

The following example, written in pseudocode, is intended to show how a memory leak can come about, and its effects, without needing any programming knowledge. The program in this case is part of some very simple software designed to control an elevator. This part of the program is run whenever anyone inside the elevator presses the button for a floor.

```
When a button is pressed:
  Get some memory, which will be used to remember the floor number
  Put the floor number into the memory
  Are we already on the target floor?
    If so, we have nothing to do: finished
    Otherwise:
      Wait until the lift is idle
      Go to the required floor
      Release the memory we used to remember the floor number
```

The memory leak would occur if the floor number requested is the same floor that the lift is on; the condition for releasing the memory would be skipped. Each time this case occurs, more memory is leaked.

Cases like this wouldn't usually have any immediate effects. People do not often press the button for the floor they are already on, and in any case, the lift might have enough spare memory that this could happen hundreds or thousands of times. However, the lift will eventually run out of memory. This could take months or years, so it might not be discovered by thorough testing.

The consequences would be unpleasant; at the very least, the lift would stop responding to requests to move to another floor. If other parts of the program need memory — a part assigned to open and close the door, for example —, then someone may be trapped inside, since the software cannot open the door.

The memory leak lasts until the system is reset. For example: if the lift's power were turned off the program would stop running. When power was turned on again, the program would restart and all the memory would be available again, but the slow process of memory leak would restart together with the program, eventually prejudicing the correct running of the system.

Programming issues

Memory leaks are a common error in programming, especially when using languages that have no built-in automatic garbage collection, such as C and C++. Typically, a memory leak occurs because dynamically allocated memory has become unreachable. The prevalence of memory leak bugs has led to the development of a number of debugging tools to detect unreachable memory. *IBM Rational Purify*, *BoundsChecker*, *Valgrind*, *Insure++* and *memwatch* are some of the more popular memory debuggers for C and C++ programs. "Conservative" garbage collection capabilities can be added to any programming language that lacks it as a built-in feature, and libraries for doing this are available for C and C++ programs. A conservative collector finds and reclaims most, but not all, unreachable memory.

Although the memory manager can recover unreachable memory, it cannot free memory that is still reachable and therefore potentially still useful. Modern memory managers therefore provide techniques for programmers to semantically mark memory with varying levels of usefulness, which correspond to varying levels of *reachability*. The memory manager does not free an object that is strongly reachable. An object is strongly reachable if it is reachable either directly by a strong reference or indirectly by a chain of strong references. (A *strong reference* is a reference that, unlike a weak reference, prevents an object from being garbage collected.) To prevent this, the developer is responsible for cleaning up references after use, typically by setting the reference to null once it is no longer needed and, if necessary, by deregistering any event listeners that maintain strong references to the object.

In general, automatic memory management is more robust and convenient for developers, as they don't need to implement freeing routines or worry about the sequence in which cleanup is performed or be concerned about whether or not an object is still referenced. It is easier for a programmer to know when a reference is no longer needed than to know when an object is no longer referenced. However, automatic memory management can impose a performance overhead, and it does not eliminate all of the programming errors that cause memory leaks.

RAII

RAII, short for Resource Acquisition Is Initialization, is an approach to the problem commonly taken in C++, D, and Ada. It involves associating scoped objects with the acquired resources, and automatically releasing the resources once the objects are out of scope. Unlike garbage collection, RAII has the advantage of knowing when objects exist and when not. Compare the following C and C++ examples:

```
/* C version */
#include <stdlib.h>

void f(int n)
{
```

```
    int* array = calloc(n, sizeof(int));
    do_some_work();
    free(array);
}

// C++ version
#include <vector>

void f(int n)
{
    std::vector<int> array (n);
    do_some_work();
}
```

The C version, as implemented in the example, requires explicit deallocation; the array is allocated from the heap, and continues to exist until explicitly freed.

The C++ version requires no explicit deallocation; it will always occur automatically as soon as the object array goes out of scope, including if an exception is thrown. This avoids the overhead of garbage collection schemes, and can even be applied to resources other than memory such as:

- file handles, which mark-and-sweep garbage collection does not handle as gracefully
- windows that have to be closed
- icons in the notification area that have to be hidden
- synchronisation primitives like monitors, critical sections, etc. which must be released to allow other threads to obtain them
- Windows registry handles that are open
- network connections
- Windows GDI objects
- Actions to perform when a function (or code block) finishes, at any possible point (the action is done by the destructor of an object created when the function starts)

However, using RAII correctly is not always easy and has its own pitfalls. For instance, if one is not careful, it is possible to create dangling pointers (or references) by returning data by reference, only to have that data be deleted when its containing object goes out of scope.

D uses a combination of RAII and garbage collection, employing automatic destruction when it is clear that an object cannot be accessed outside its original scope, and garbage collection otherwise.

Reference counting and cyclic references

More modern garbage collection schemes are often based on a notion of reachability - if you don't have a usable reference to the memory in question, it can be collected. Other garbage collection schemes can be based on reference counting, where an object is responsible for keeping track of how many references are pointing to it. If the number goes down to zero, the object is expected to release itself and allow its memory to be reclaimed. The flaw with this model is that it doesn't cope with cyclic references, and this is why nowadays we are prepared to accept the burden of the more costly mark and sweep type of systems.

The following code illustrates the canonical reference-counting memory leak.

```
Dim A, B
Set A = CreateObject("Some.Thing")
Set B = CreateObject("Some.Thing")
```

```
' At this point, the two objects each have one reference,
Set A.member = B
Set B.member = A
' Now they each have two references.
Set A = Nothing
' You could still get out of it...
Set B = Nothing
' You now have a memory leak.
```

In practice, this trivial example would be spotted straight away and fixed. In most real examples, the cycle of references spans more than two objects, and is more difficult to detect.

A well-known example of this kind of leak came to prominence with the rise of AJAX programming techniques in web browsers. Javascript code which associated a DOM element with an event handler and failed to remove the reference before exiting, would leak memory (AJAX web pages keep a given DOM alive for a lot longer than traditional web pages, so this leak was much more apparent).

Effects

If a program has a memory leak and its memory usage is steadily increasing, there will not usually be an immediate symptom. Every physical system has a finite amount of memory, and if the memory leak is not contained (for example, by restarting the program with the leak) it will sooner or later start to cause problems.

Most modern consumer desktop operating systems have both main memory which is physically housed in RAM microchips, and secondary storage such as a hard drive. Memory allocation is dynamic - each process gets as much memory as it requests. Active pages are transferred into main memory for fast access; inactive pages are pushed out to secondary storage to make room, as needed. When a single process starts consuming a large amount of memory, it usually occupies more and more of main memory, pushing other programs out to secondary storage - usually significantly slowing performance of the system. Even if the leaking program is terminated, it may take some time for other programs to swap back into main memory, and for performance to return to normal.

When all the memory on a system is exhausted (whether there is virtual memory or only main memory, such as on an embedded system) any attempt to allocate more memory will fail. This usually causes the program attempting to allocate the memory to terminate itself, or to generate a segmentation fault. Some programs are designed to recover from this situation (possibly by falling back on pre-reserved memory). The first program to experience the out-of-memory may or may not be the program that has the memory leak.

Some multi-tasking operating systems have special mechanisms to deal with an out-of-memory condition, such as killing processes at random (which may affect "innocent" processes), or killing the largest process in memory (which presumably is the one causing the problem). Some operating systems have a per-process memory limit, to prevent any one program from hogging all of the memory on the system. The disadvantage to this arrangement is that the operating system sometimes must be re-configured to allow proper operation of programs that legitimately require large amounts of memory, such as those dealing with graphics, video, or scientific calculations.

If the memory leak is in the kernel, the operating system itself will likely fail. Computers without sophisticated memory management, such as embedded systems, may also completely fail from a persistent memory leak.

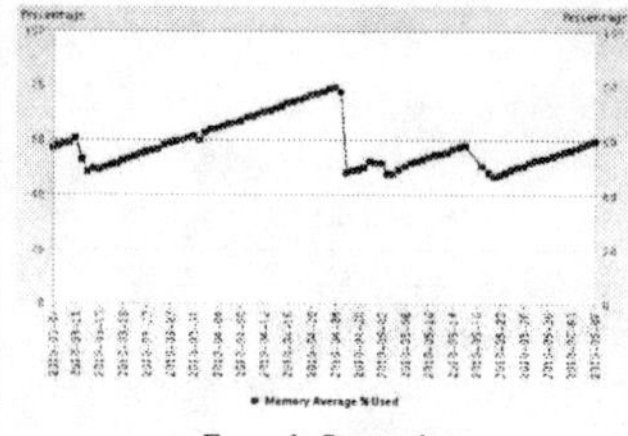
Example Sawtooth.

Publicly accessible systems such as web servers or routers are prone to denial-of-service attacks if an attacker discovers a sequence of operations which can trigger a leak. Such a sequence is known as an exploit.

A "sawtooth" pattern of memory utilization may be an indicator of a memory leak if the vertical drops coincide with reboots or application restarts. Care should be taken though because Garbage Collection points could also cause such a pattern.

Other memory consumers

Note that constantly increasing memory usage is not necessarily evidence of a memory leak. Some applications will store ever increasing amounts of information in memory (e.g. as a cache). If the cache can grow so large as to cause problems, this may be a programming or design error, but is not a memory leak as the information remains nominally in use. In other cases, programs may require an unreasonably large amount of memory because the programmer has assumed memory is always sufficient for a particular task; for example, a graphics file processor might start by reading the entire contents of an image file and storing it all into memory, something that is not viable where a very large image exceeds available memory.

To put it another way, a memory leak arises from a particular kind of programming error, and without access to the program code, someone seeing symptoms can only guess that there *might* be a memory leak. It would be better to use terms such as "constantly increasing memory use" where no such inside knowledge exists.

A simple example in C

The following C function deliberately leaks memory by losing the pointer to the allocated memory. Since the program loops forever calling the memory allocation function, malloc(), but without saving the address, it will eventually fail (returning NULL) when no more memory is available to the program. Because the address of each allocation is not stored, it is impossible to free any of the previously allocated blocks. It should be noted that, generally, the operating system delays real memory allocation until something is written into it. So the program ends when virtual addresses run out of bounds (per process limits or 2 to 4 GiB on IA-32 or a lot more on x86-64 systems) and there may be no real impact on the rest of the system.

```
#include <stdlib.h>

int main(void)
{
     /* this is an infinite loop calling the malloc function which
      * allocates the memory but without saving the address of the
      * allocated place */
     while (malloc(50)); /* malloc will return NULL sooner or later,
due to lack of memory */
     return 0;  /* free the allocated memory by operating system itself
 after program exits */
}
```

See also

- Buffer overflow
- Handle leak
- Memory management
- Memory debugger

References

- Detecting a Memory Leak (http://msdn2.microsoft.com/en-us/library/Aa293901(VS.60).aspx) (Using MFC Debugging Support)
- Article " Memory Leak Detection in C++ (http://linuxjournal.com/article.php?sid=6556)" by Cal Erickson
- Article " Memory Leak Detection in Embedded Systems (http://linuxjournal.com/article.php?sid=6059)" by Cal Erickson
- Why doesn't my application release the memory? (http://jb2works.com/memoryleak/index.html) (Java FAQ)
- Article " Fixing Memory Leaks in KDE (http://developer.kde.org/documentation/other/memoryleaks.html)" by Harri Porten
- Article " Finding and Fixing Memory Leaks (http://bravobug.com/news/?p=116) on Mac OS X"
- Resolving memory leaks (http://www.rt-embedded.com/blog/archives/memory-leaks/), an article from the Real-Time embedded blog.

NaN

In computing, **NaN** (**N**ot **a** **N**umber) is a value of numeric data type representing an undefined or unrepresentable value, especially in floating-point calculations. Systematic use of NaNs was introduced by the IEEE 754 floating-point standard in 1985, along with the representation of other non-finite quantities like infinities.

Two separate kinds of NaNs are provided, termed quiet NaNs and signaling NaNs. Quiet NaNs are used to propagate errors resulting from invalid operations or values, whereas signaling NaNs can support advanced features such as mixing numerical and symbolic computation or other extensions to basic floating-point arithmetic. For example, 0/0 is undefined as a real number, and so represented by NaN; the square root of a negative number is imaginary, and thus not representable as a real floating-point number, and so is represented by NaN; and NaNs may be used to represent missing values in computations[1] [2]

Floating point

In floating-point calculations, NaN is not the same as infinity, although both are typically handled as special cases in floating-point representations of real numbers as well as in floating-point operations. An invalid operation is also not the same as an arithmetic overflow (which might return an infinity) or an arithmetic underflow (which would return the smallest normal number, a denormal number, or zero).

IEEE 754 NaNs are represented with the exponential field filled with ones and some non-zero number in the significand. A bit-wise example of a IEEE floating-point standard single precision (32-bit) NaN: s111 1111 1axx xxxx xxxx xxxx xxxx xxxx where *s* is the sign, *x* is the payload, and *a* determines the type of NaN. If $a = 1$, it is a **quiet NaN**; if *a* is zero and the payload is nonzero, then it is a **signaling NaN**[3] .

Floating point operations other than comparisons normally propagate a quiet NaN (*qNaN*). Floating point operations on a signaling NaN (*sNaN*) signal an invalid operation exception, the default exception action is then the same as for qNaN operands and they produce a qNaN if producing a floating point result.

A comparison with a NaN always returns an *unordered result* even when comparing with itself. The comparison predicates are either signaling or non-signaling, the signaling versions signal an invalid exception for such comparisons. The equality and inequality predicates are non-signaling so $x = x$ returning false can be used to test if x is a quiet NaN. The other standard comparison predicates all signal if they receive a NaN operand, the standard also provides non-signaling versions of these other predicates. The predicate *isNaN(x)* determines if a value is a NaN and never signals an exception.

The propagation of quiet NaNs through arithmetic operations enables errors to be detected at the end of a sequence of operations without extensive testing during intermediate stages.

In the revised IEEE 754-2008 standard there are a few anomalous functions (such as the **maxnum** function, which returns the maximum of two operands which are expected to be numbers) favor numbers—if just one of the operands is a NaN then the value of the other operand is returned.

The NaN 'toolbox' [4] for GNU Octave and MATLAB goes one step further and skips all NaNs. NaNs are *assumed* to represent missing values and so the statistical functions ignore NaNs in the data instead of propagating them. Every computation in the NaN toolbox is based on the non-NaN data only.

Creation

There are three kinds of operation which return NaN:[5]

- Operations with a NaN as at least one operand
- Indeterminate forms
  - The divisions $0/0$, ∞/∞, $\infty/-\infty$, $-\infty/\infty$, and $-\infty/-\infty$
  - The multiplications $0\times\infty$ and $0\times-\infty$
  - The additions $\infty + (-\infty)$, $(-\infty) + \infty$ and equivalent subtractions
  - The standard has alternative functions for powers:
    - The standard `pow` function and the integer exponent `pown` function define 0^0, 1^∞, and ∞^0 as 1.
    - The `powr` function define all three indeterminate forms as invalid operations and so returns NaN.
- Real operations with complex results, for example:
  - The square root of a negative number
  - The logarithm of a negative number
  - The inverse sine or cosine of a number which is less than -1 or greater than $+1$.

NaNs may also be explicitly assigned to variables, typically as a representation for missing values. Prior to the IEEE standard, programmers often used a special value (such as −99999999) to represent undefined or missing values, but there was no guarantee that they would be handled consistently or correctly.[1]

NaNs are not necessarily generated by the processor. In the case of quiet NaNs, the first item is always valid for each processor; the others may not necessarily be. For example, on the Intel Architecture processors, the FPU *never* creates a NaN except in the first case, unless the corresponding floating point exception mask bits have been set.[6] The other items would cause exceptions, not NaNs. However, the software exception handler may examine the operands and decide to return a NaN (e.g. in the case of 0/0).

Quiet NaN

Quiet NaNs, or qNaNs, do not raise any additional exceptions as they propagate through most operations. The exceptions are where the NaN cannot simply be passed through unchanged to the output, such as in format conversions or certain comparison operations (which do not "expect" a NaN input).

Signaling NaN

Signaling NaNs, or sNaNs, are special forms of a NaN which when consumed by most operations should raise an invalid exception and then, if appropriate, be "quieted" into a qNaN which may then propagate. They were introduced in IEEE 754. There have been several ideas for how these might be used:

- Filling uninitialized memory with signaling NaNs would produce an invalid exception if the data is used before it is initialized
- Using an sNaN as a placeholder for a more complicated object, such as:
  - A representation of a number that has underflowed
  - A representation of a number that has overflowed
  - Number in a higher precision format
  - A complex number

When encountered a trap handler could decode the sNaN and return an index to the computed result. In practice this approach is faced with many complications. The treatment of the sign bit of NaNs for some simple operations (such as absolute value) is different from that for arithmetic operations. Traps are not required by the standard. There are other approaches to this sort of problem which would be more portable.

Function definition

There are differences of opinion about the proper definition for the result of a numeric function which receives a (quiet) NaN as input. One view is that the NaN should propagate to the output of the function in all cases to propagate the indication of an error. Another view is that if the function has multiple arguments and the output is uniquely determined by all the non-NaN inputs, then that value should be the result.

```
If we define pow(x,y) = x ** y
What is pow(1, NaN)?
```

The first view is that the output should be NaN since one of the inputs is. The second view is that since pow(1, y) = 1 for any real number y, or even if y is infinity or -infinity, then it is appropriate to return 1 for the case of pow(1, NaN). This is the approach in many math libraries. However 1^{∞} is an indeterminate form, a limit of this form can tend to any number or infinity, and therefore NaN is a better answer in some circumstances. The IEEE 754 standard says that the value of functions at singular points can be taken as a particular value if that value is in the limit the value for all but a vanishingly small part of a ball around the parameters. With this reasoning they have determined that `pow(0,0)` for instance should be set to 1.

Integer NaN

Most fixed sized integer formats do not have any way of explicitly indicating invalid data.

Perl's BigInt package uses "NaN" for the result of strings which don't represent valid integers.

```
>perl -mMath::BigInt -e "print Math::BigInt->new('foo')"
NaN
```

Display

Different operating systems and programming languages may have different string representations of NaN.

```
nan
NaN
NaN%
NAN
NaNQ
NaNS
qNaN
sNaN
1.#SNAN
1.#QNAN
-1.#IND
```

Since, in practice, encoded NaNs have both a sign and optional 'diagnostic information' (sometimes called a *payload*), these will often be found in string representations of NaNs, too, for example:

```
-NaN
 NaN12345
-sNaN12300
```

(other variants exist)

Encoding

In IEEE 754 standard-conform floating point storage formats, NaNs are identified by specific, pre-defined bit patterns unique to NaNs and that cannot be inadvertently mistaken for regular (defined and representable) floating point values.

- In all four binary formats (b16, b32, b64, b128), NaNs are identified by

1. an exponent field in which all bits are non-zero (like the storage format for ±infinity) *and*
2. a fraction field in which at least one bit is non-zero (unlike the storage format for ±infinity).

   In practice, signaled/quiet state is represented in the first bit following the sign and exponent fields. (on both big- and little-endian systems, this is the most significant bit in the fraction field). The exact interpretation of that bit varies (see below). When the quiet/signaling bit is clear at least one other bit in the fraction field will/must be set to ensure that the encoding for NaNs is distinguishable from the encoding for ±infinity.

- In all three decimal formats (d32, d64, d128), NaNs are identified by

1. five non-zero bits following the sign bit.

   Signaled/quiet state is represented in the sixth bit following the sign bit.

These patterns are independent of precision. They are also used in non-standard but IEEE 754-like floating point formats such as Intel's/Motorola's 80bit "extended precision" or 8bit "minifloats".

The original IEEE 754 standard from 1985 (IEEE 754-1985) did not specify how the signaled/quiet state was to be tagged. Two different implementations, with reversed meanings, resulted.

- most processors (including those of the Intel/AMD x86-32/x86-64 family, the Motorola 68000 family, the AIM PowerPC family, the ARM family, and the Sun SPARC family) set the signaled/quiet bit to non-zero if the NaN is quiet, and to zero if the NaN is signaling. Thus, on these processors, the bit represents an 'is_quiet' flag.
- in NaNs generated by the PA-RISC and MIPS processors, the signaled/quiet bit is zero if the NaN is quiet, and non-zero if the NaN is signaling. Thus, on these processors, the bit represents an 'is_signaling' flag.

The 2008 revision of the IEEE 754 standard (IEEE 754-2008) makes formal recommendations for the interpretation of the signaled/quiet bit.

- For binary formats, the standard follows the interpretation as an 'is_quiet' flag. I.e. the signaled/quiet bit is non-zero if the NaN is quiet, and zero if the NaN is signaling. The standard still allows implementations to use several bits to distinguish signaling and quiet NaNs.
- For decimal formats, the standard follows the interpretation as an 'is_signaling' flag. I.e. the signaled/quiet bit is zero if the NaN is quiet, and non-zero if the NaN is signaling.

The state/value of the remaining bits (i.e. other than the ones used to identify a NaN as NaN, including the quiet/signaled bits) are not defined by the standard.

References

[1] Bowman, Kenneth (2006) An introduction to programming with IDL: Interactive Data Language. Academic Press. p. 26 ISBN 012088559X

[2] William H. Press, Saul A. Teukolsky, William T. Vetterling (2007) Numerical recipes: the art of scientific computing.p. 34 Cambridge University Press, ISBN 0521880688

[3] If *a* is zero and the payload is zero, then it represents infinity.

[4] http://www.dpmi.tu-graz.ac.at/~schloegl/matlab/NaN/

[5] David Goldberg. "What Every Computer Scientist Should Know About Floating-Point" (http://docs.sun.com/source/806-3568/ncg_goldberg.html). .

[6] "Intel 64 and IA-32 Architectures Software Developer's Manual Volume 1: Basic Architecture" (http://www.intel.com/products/processor/manuals/index.htm). April 2008. pp. 118–125, 266–267, 334–335. .

External links

- http://foldoc.org/?Not-a-Number
- IEEE 754-2008 Standard for Floating-Point Arithmetic (http://ieeexplore.ieee.org/servlet/opac?punumber=4610933) (requires login / not free)

Negative cache

In computer programming, **negative cache** is a cache that also stores "negative" responses, i.e. failures. This means that a program remembers the result indicating a failure even after the cause has been corrected. Usually negative cache is a design choice, but it can also be a software bug.

Examples

Consider a web browser which attempts to load a page while the network is unavailable. The browser will receive an error code indicating the problem, and may display this error message to the user in place of the requested page. However, it is incorrect for the browser to place the error message in the page cache, as this would lead it to display the error again when the user tries to load the same page - even after the network is back up. The error message must not be cached under the page's URL; until the browser is able to successfully load the page, whenever the user tries to load the page, the browser must make a new attempt.

A frustrating aspect of negative caches is that the user may put a great effort into troubleshooting the problem, and then after determining and removing the root cause, the error still does not vanish.

There are cases where failure-like states must be cached. For instance, DNS requires that caching nameservers remember negative responses as well as positive ones. If an authoritative nameserver returns a negative response, indicating that a name does not exist, this is cached. The negative response may be perceived as a failure at the application level; however, to the nameserver caching it, it is not a failure. The cache times for negative and positive caching may be tuned independently.

Description

A negative cache is normally only desired if failure is very expensive and the error condition arises automatically without user's action. It creates a situation where the user is unable to isolate the cause of the failure: despite fixing everything he/she can think of, the program still refuses to work. When a failure is cached, the program should provide a clear indication of what must be done to clear the cache, in addition to a description of the cause of the error. In such conditions a negative cache is an example of a design anti-pattern.

See also

- Perl Design Patterns Book

Software aging

Software aging refers to progressive performance degradation or a sudden hang/crash of a software system due to exhaustion of operating system resources, fragmentation and accumulation of errors. A proactive fault management method to deal with the software aging phenomenon is software rejuvenation. This method can be classified as an environment diversity technique that usually is implemented through software rejuvenation agents (SRA).

References

[1] M. Grottke, L. Li, K. Vaidyanathan, and K.S. Trivedi, "Analysis of software aging in a web server," IEEE Transactions on Reliability, vol. 55, no. 3, pp. 411-420, 2006.

[2] R. Matias Jr. and P. J. Freitas Filho, "An experimental study on software aging and rejuvenation in web servers," Proceedings of the 30th Annual International Computer Software and Applications Conference (COMPSAC'06), Vol. 01, pp. 189 - 196, 2006.

[3] M. Grottke and K. S. Trivedi "Fighting bugs: Remove, retry, replicate and rejuvenate," IEEE Computer, vol. 40, no. 2, pp. 107–109, 2007.

[4] M. Grottke, R. Matias Jr., and K. S. Trivedi "The Fundamentals of Software Aging," Workshop of Software Aging and Rejuvenation (WoSAR/ISSRE), 2008.

Stack buffer overflow

In software, a **stack buffer overflow** occurs when a program writes to a memory address on the program's call stack outside of the intended data structure; usually a fixed length buffer.[1] [2] Stack buffer overflow bugs are caused when a program writes more data to a buffer located on the stack than there was actually allocated for that buffer. This almost always results in corruption of adjacent data on the stack, and in cases where the overflow was triggered by mistake, will often cause the program to crash or operate incorrectly. This type of overflow is part of the more general class of programming bugs known as buffer overflows.[1]

If the affected program is running with special privileges, or accepts data from untrusted network hosts (e.g. a webserver) then the bug is a potential security vulnerability. If the stack buffer is filled with data supplied from an untrusted user then that user can corrupt the stack in such a way as to inject executable code into the running program and take control of the process. This is one of the oldest and more reliable methods for hackers to gain unauthorized access to a computer.[3] [4] [5]

Exploiting stack buffer overflows

The canonical method for exploiting a stack based buffer overflow is to overwrite the function return address with a pointer to attacker-controlled data (usually on the stack itself).[3] [6] This is illustrated in the example below:

An example with strcpy

```
#include <string.h>

void foo (char *bar)
{
   char  c[12];

   strcpy(c, bar);  // no bounds checking...
```

```
}

int main (int argc, char **argv)
{
   foo(argv[1]);
}
```

This code takes an argument from the command line and copies it to a local stack variable c. This works fine for command line arguments smaller than 12 characters (as you can see in figure B below). Any arguments larger than 11 characters long will result in corruption of the stack. (The maximum number of characters that is safe is one less than the size of the buffer here because in the C programming language strings are delimited by a zero byte character. A twelve-character input thus requires thirteen bytes to store, the input followed by the sentinel zero byte. The zero byte then ends up overwriting a memory location that's one byte beyond the end of the buffer.)

The program stack in foo() with various inputs

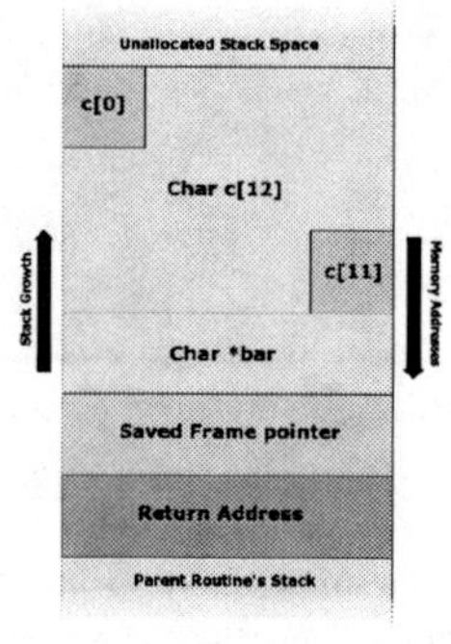

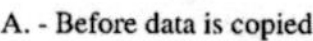

A. - Before data is copied.

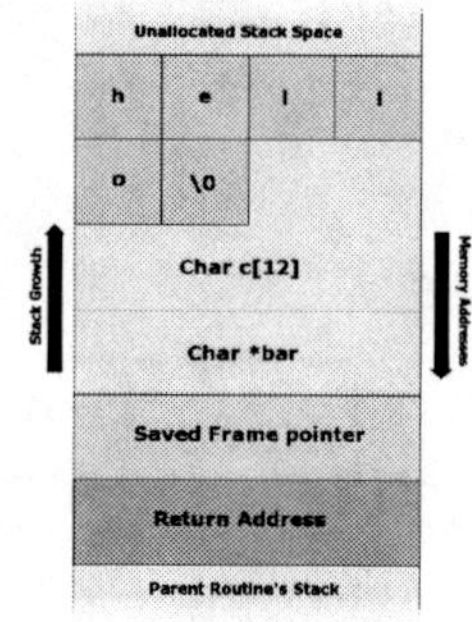

B. - "hello" is the first command line argument.

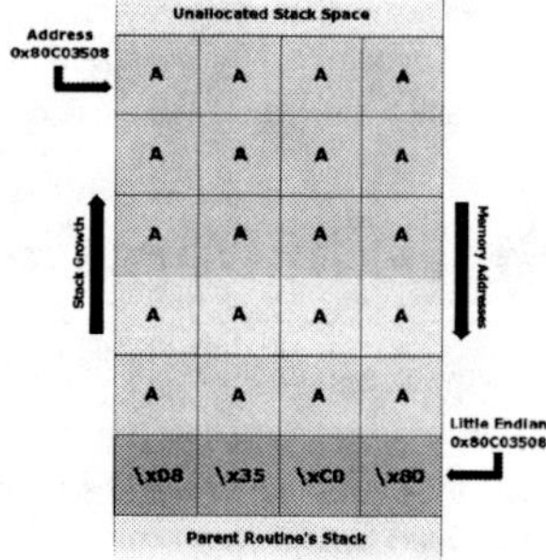

C. - "A A A A A A A A A A A A A A A A A A A A \x08 \x35 \xC0 \x80" is the first command line argument.

Notice in figure C above, when an argument larger than 11 bytes is supplied on the command line foo() overwrites local stack data, the saved frame pointer, and most importantly, the return address. When foo() returns it pops the return address off the stack and jumps to that address (i.e. starts executing instructions from that address). As you can see in figure C above, the attacker has overwritten the return address with a pointer to the stack buffer char c[12], which now contains attacker supplied data. In an actual stack buffer overflow exploit the string of "A"'s would be replaced with shellcode suitable to the platform and desired function. If this program had special privileges (e.g. the SUID bit set to run as the superuser), then the attacker could use this vulnerability to gain superuser privileges on the affected machine.[3]

The attacker also can modify internal variables values to exploit some bugs. With same example :

```
#include <string.h>
#include <stdio.h>

void foo (char *bar)
{
   float My_Float = 10.5; // Addr = 0x0023FF4C
```

```
   char  c[12];             // Addr = 0x0023FF30

   // Will print 10.500000
   printf("My Float value = %f\n", My_Float);

    /* --------------------------------------------------------
      Memory map:
      @ : c allocated memory
      # : My_Float allocated memory
      - : other memory

         *c                              *My_Float
      0x0023FF30                        0x0023FF4C
         |                                  |
         @@@@@@@@@@@@-----------------#####
     foo("my string is too long !!!!! XXXXX");

   memcpy will put 0x1010C042 in My_Float value.
   ---------------------------------------------------------*/

   memcpy(c, bar, strlen(bar));  // no bounds checking...

   // Will print 96.031372
   printf("My Float value = %f\n", My_Float);
}

int main (int argc, char **argv)
{
   foo("my string is too long !!!!! \x10\x10\xC0\x42");
   return 0;
}
```

Platform related differences

A number of platforms have subtle differences in their implementation of the call stack that can affect the way a stack buffer overflow exploit will work. Some machine architectures store the top level return address of the call stack in a register. This means that any overwritten return address will not be used until a later unwinding of the call stack. Another example of a machine specific detail that can affect the choice of exploitation techniques is the fact that most RISC style machine architectures will not allow unaligned access to memory.[7] Combined with a fixed length for machine opcodes this machine limitation can make the jump to ESP technique almost impossible to implement (with the one exception being when the program actually contains the unlikely code to explicitly jump to the stack register).[8] [9]

Stacks that grow up

Within the topic of stack buffer overflows, an often discussed but rarely seen architecture is one in which the stack grows in the opposite direction. This change in architecture is frequently suggested as a solution to the stack buffer overflow problem because any overflow of a stack buffer that occurs within the same stack frame can not overwrite the return pointer. Further investigation of this claimed protection finds it to be a naive solution at best. Any overflow that occurs in a buffer from a previous stack frame will still overwrite a return pointer and allow for malicious exploitation of the bug.[10] For instance, in the example above, the return pointer for foo will not be overwritten because the overflow actually occurs within the stack frame for strcpy. However, because the buffer that overflows during the call to strcpy resides in a previous stack frame, the return pointer for strcpy will have a numerically higher memory address than the buffer. This means that instead of the return pointer for foo being overwritten, the return pointer for strcpy will be overwritten. At most this means that growing the stack in the opposite direction will change some details of how stack buffer overflows are exploitable, but it will not reduce significantly in the number of exploitable bugs.

Protection schemes

Over the years a number of schemes have been developed to inhibit malicious stack buffer overflow exploitation. These usually have taken one of two forms. The first method is to detect that a stack buffer overflow has occurred and thus prevent redirection of the instruction pointer to malicious code. The second attempts to prevent the execution of malicious code from the stack without directly detecting the stack buffer overflow.[11]

Stack canaries

Stack canaries, so named because they operate as a canary in a coal mine so to speak, are used to detect a stack buffer overflow before execution of malicious code can occur. This method works by placing a small integer, the value of which is randomly chosen at program start, in memory just before the stack return pointer. Most buffer overflows overwrite memory from lower to higher memory addresses, so in order to overwrite the return pointer (and thus take control of the process) the canary value must also be overwritten. This value is checked to make sure it has not changed before a routine uses the return pointer on the stack.[2] This technique can greatly increase the difficulty of exploiting a stack buffer overflow because it forces the attacker to gain control of the instruction pointer by some nontraditional means such as corrupting other important variables on the stack.[2]

Nonexecutable stack

Another approach to preventing stack buffer overflow exploitation is to enforce memory policy on stack memory region to disallow execution from the stack. This means that in order to execute shellcode from the stack an attacker must either find a way to disable the execution protection from memory, or find a way to put his shellcode payload in a non-protected region of memory. This method is becoming more popular now that hardware support for the no-execute flag is available in most desktop processors. While this method definitely makes the canonical approach to stack buffer overflow exploitation fail it is not without its problems. First it is common to find ways to store shellcode in unprotected memory regions like the heap, and so very little need change in the way of exploitation.[12] Even if this were not so, there are other ways. The most damning is the so called return to libc method for shellcode creation. In this attack the malicious payload will load the stack not with shellcode, but with a proper call stack so that execution is vectored to a chain of standard library calls, usually with the effect of disabling memory execute protections and allowing shellcode to run as normal.[13] This works because the execution never actually vectors to the stack itself. Still if used in conjunction with techniques like ASLR a nonexecutable stack can be somewhat resistant to return to libc attacks and thus can greatly improve the security of an application.

Notable examples

- The Morris worm spread in part by exploiting a stack buffer overflow in the Unix finger server.[14]
- The Witty worm spread by exploiting a stack buffer overflow in the Internet Security Systems BlackICE Desktop Agent.[15]
- The Slammer worm spread by exploiting a stack buffer overflow in Microsoft's SQL server.[16]
- The Blaster worm spread by exploiting a stack buffer overflow in Microsoft DCOM service
- The Twilight hack was made for the Wii by giving a lengthy character name for the horse ('Epona') in The Legend of Zelda: Twilight Princess. This caused a stack buffer overflow, allowing arbitrary code to be run on an unmodified system.

See also

- Address space layout randomization
- Buffer overflow
- Call stack
- Computer security
- ExecShield
- Executable_space_protection
- Exploit (computer security)
- Format string attack
- grsecurity
- Heap overflow
- Integer overflow
- NX bit
- PaX
- Return-oriented programming
- Security-Enhanced_Linux
- Stack overflow
- storage violation
- Vulnerability (computing)

References

[1] Fithen, William L; Seacord, Robert (2007-03-27). "VT-MB. Violation of Memory Bounds" (https://www.securecoding.cert.org/confluence/display/sci/VT-MB.+Violation+of+Memory+Bounds). US CERT. .

[2] Dowd, Mark; McDonald, John; Schuh, Justin (November 2006). *The Art Of Software Security Assessment*. Addison Wesley. pp. 169–196. ISBN 0-321-44442-6.

[3] Levy, Elias (1996-11-08). "Smashing the stack for fun and profit" (http://www.phrack.org/issues.html?issue=49&id=14&mode=txt). *Phrack* **7** (49): 14. .

[4] Pincus, Jonathan; Baker, Brandon (July-August 2004). "Beyond Stack Smashing: Recent Advances in Exploiting Buffer Overruns" (http://research.microsoft.com/users/jpincus/beyond-stack-smashing.pdf) (– Scholar search (http://scholar.google.co.uk/scholar?hl=en&lr=&q=author:+intitle:Beyond+Stack+Smashing:+Recent+Advances+in+Exploiting+Buffer+Overruns&as_publication=IEEE+Security+&+Privacy&as_ylo=&as_yhi=&btnG=Search)). *IEEE Security & Privacy* **2** (4): 20–27. doi:10.1109/MSP.2004.36. .

[5] Burebista (PDF). *Stack Overflows* (http://www.securityforest.com/downloads/educationtree/stack_overflows.pdf). .

[6] Bertrand, Louis (2002). "OpenBsd: Fix the Bugs, Secure the System" (http://www.openbsd.org/slides/musess_2002/img16.htm). . .

[7] pr1 (HTML). *Exploiting SPARC Buffer Overflow vulnerabilities* (http://www.utdallas.edu/~edsha/UGsecurity/sparcoverflow.htm). .

[8] Curious (2005-01-08). "Reverse engineering - PowerPC Cracking on Mac OS X with GDB" (http://www.phrack.org/issues.html?issue=63&id=16#article). *Phrack* **11** (63): 16. .

[9] Sovarel, Ana Nora; Evans, David; Paul, Nathanael (HTML). *Where's the FEEB? The Effectiveness of Instruction Set Randomization* (http://www.cs.virginia.edu/feeb/paper/). .

[10] Zhodiac (2001-12-28). "HP-UX (PA-RISC 1.1) Overflows" (http://www.trust-us.ch/phrack/show.php@p=58&a=11). *Phrack* **11** (58): 11. .

[11] Ward, Craig E. (2005-06-13). "C/C++ Buffer Overflows" (http://homepage.mac.com/cewcew/talks/buffer-overflows/cew-uuasc20050613-revised.pdf) (PDF). . Orange County, California. .
[12] Foster, James C.; Osipov, Vitaly; Bhalla, Nish; Heinen, Niels (2005) (PDF). *Buffer Overflow Attacks: Detect, Exploit, Prevent* (http://apossum.alfaspace.net/eng/Syngress.Buffer.Overflow.Attacks.Dec.2004.ISBN1932266674.pdf). United States of America: Syngress Publishing,Inc.. ISBN 1-932266-67-4. .
[13] Nergal (2001-12-28). "The advanced return-into-lib(c) exploits: PaX case study" (http://www.phrack.org/issues.html?issue=58&id=4#article). *Phrack* **11** (58): 4. .
[14] http://www.ee.ryerson.ca/~elf/hack/iworm.html
[15] http://www.icsi.berkeley.edu/~nweaver/login_witty.txt
[16] http://www.wired.com/wired/archive/11.07/slammer.html

Stale pointer bug

A **stale pointer bug**, otherwise known as an **aliasing bug**, is a class of subtle programming errors that can arise in code that does dynamic memory allocation, especially via the malloc function or equivalent.

If several pointers address (are "aliases for") a given hunk of storage, it may happen that the storage is freed or reallocated (and thus moved) through one alias and then referenced through another, which may lead to subtle (and possibly intermittent) lossage depending on the state and the allocation history of the malloc arena. This bug can be avoided by never creating aliases for allocated memory, by controlling the dynamic scope of references to the storage so that none can remain when it is freed, or by use of a garbage collector, in the form of an intelligent memory-allocation library or as provided by higher-level languages, such as Lisp.

The term "aliasing bug" is nowadays associated with C programming, but it was already in use in a very similar sense in the ALGOL 60 and Fortran programming language communities in the 1960s.

See also

- Dangling pointer

Article Sources and Contributors

Lightweight software test automation *Source*: http://en.wikipedia.org/w/index.php?oldid=243629142 *Contributors*: Colonies Chris, Greenrd, JamesDmccaffrey, John Vandenberg, OracleDBGuru, Torc2, Tutterz, Verbal, 9 anonymous edits

Computer programs *Source*: http://en.wikipedia.org/w/index.php?oldid=16233864 *Contributors*: 16@r, ABF, AKGhetto, AVRS, Abdullais4u, Adrianwn, AdultSwim, Ahoerstemeier, Airada, Alansohn, Aldaron, Aldie, Ale jrb, AlefZet, Aleksd, Alisha0512, AlistairMcMillan, Allan McInnes, Ancheta Wis, Andre Engels, Andrejj, Andres, Animum, Anja98, Ans-mo, Antandrus, Ash211, Atlant, Barkingdoc, Barts1a, Bfinn, Bhadani, Blainster, Boothy443, Born2cycle, Bornhj, Bryan Derksen, Can't sleep, clown will eat me, CanadianLinuxUser, Cap'n Refsmmat, CardinalDan, Cartiman, Children.of.the.Kron, Chriswiki, Chun-hian, CommonsDelinker, Conversion script, CopperMurdoch, CurranH, Cybercobra, DMacks, Danakil, David Kernow, Deliv3ranc3, Derek farn, Dicklyon, Diego Moya, Discospinster, DonToto, Duncharris, ERobson, Edward, Ehheh, ElKevbo, Elassint, EncMstr, Enchanter, Epbr123, FF2010, Fabartus, Filemon, Firemaker117, FleetCommand, Frencheigh, Funandtrvl, Furrykef, Gaga654, Gaius Cornelius, Ghyll, Giftlite, Greenrd, Grstain, Grunt, Guppy, Gurchzilla, Guyjohnston, HappyDog, HotQuantum3000, Hu12, I'll suck anything, Ipsign, IslandHopper973, Islescape, Iulianu, JGNPILOT, JackLumber, Jackol, Jerryobject, John Fader, JohnWittle, JohnnyRush10, Jonnyapple, Josh Parris, Jotomicron, Jpbowen, Jpgordon, Jusjih, K.Nevelsteen, K.lee, KANURI SRINIVAS, Karlzt, Kdakin, Keilana, KellyCoinGuy, Kenny sh, Khalid hassani, Kusunose, Kwekubo, Larry_Sanger, Laurens-af, Lev, Liberty Miller, Liempt, Lightmouse, Ligulem, Longhair, LuchoX, Lulu of the Lotus-Eaters, Luna Santin, M, MAG1, Mac, Madhero88, Magister Mathematicae, Mani1, Manop, Martijn Hoekstra, MartinRe, Martynas Patasius, Marudubshinki, Matty4123, Maximaximax, Mermaid from the Baltic Sea, Metrax, Miguelfms, Mike Van Emmerik, Mild Bill Hiccup, Mindmatrix, Mlpkr, MmisNarifAlhoceimi, Mortenoesterlundjoergensen, Murray Langton, Nanshu, Nickokillah, Nikai, Nixdorf, Noctibus, Noosentaal, NovaSTL, Ohnoitsjamie, Oicumayberight, Oliver Pereira, Onopearls, OrgasGirl, Palnu, Paulkramer, Pearle, PetterBudt, Pharaoh of the Wizards, Philip Trueman, Poor Yorick, Power User, Proofreader77, Quota, Quuxplusone, R. S. Shaw, R. fiend, Radarjw, Radon210, Raise exception, Raven in Orbit, Rdsmith4, RedWolf, Rich Farmbrough, Rjwilmsi, Roybristow, Rusty Cashman, Ruud Koot, S.Örvarr.S, Sadi Carnot, Sannse, Saros136, Sebbb-m, Sfahey, Shanes, SigmaEpsilon, SimonD, Sir Anon, Sir Nicholas de Mimsy-Porpington, SlackerMom, Slady, Slashem, Slowking Man, Smiller933, SqlPac, Stephenb, Stevertigo, Storm Rider, Subdolous, Suisui, TakuyaMurata, Template namespace initialisation script, The Anome, The Thing That Should Not Be, Thegreenflashlight, Thingg, Thumperward, TiagoTiago, Tide rolls, Timhowardriley, Tobias Bergemann, Tobiasjwt, TomasBat, Tommy2010, TonyClarke, Troels Arvin, True Genius, Ukexpat, UrbanBard, VIKIPEDIA IS AN ANUS!, WJetChao, Welsh, Wereon, Wernher, Wesley, WhatamIdoing, Wiki alf, WikiDan61, Wikijens, Wolfkeeper, Xn4, Xp54321, Yidisheryid, Ykhwong, Yonaa, Zipircik, ZonkBB6, Zundark, Zzuuzz, 347 anonymous edits

Test automation *Source*: http://en.wikipedia.org/w/index.php?oldid=398078609 *Contributors*: 5nizza, 83nj1, ADobey, Abdull, Akr7577, AliveFreeHappy, Ameya barve, Ancheta Wis, Ankurj, Anupam naik, Apparition11, Asashour, Ash, Auntof6, Bbryson, Benjamin Geiger, Bhagat.Abhijeet, Bigtwilkins, Caltas, Carioca, Checkshirt, Chrisbepost, CodeWonk, DARTH SIDIOUS 2, DRogers, Dbelhumeur02, DivineAlpha, Dreftymac, Eaowens, EdwardMiller, Egivoni, ElfriedeDustin, Elipongo, Enoch the red, Excirial, Faris747, Ferpectionist, FlashSheridan, Flopsy Mopsy and Cottonmouth, Florian Huber, Fumitol, Gaggarwal2000, Gherget, Gibs2001, Gmacgregor, Goutham, Grafen, Harobed, Hatch68, Helix84, Hesa, Heydaysoft, Hooperbloob, Hswiki, Hu12, JASpencer, JamesBWatson, Johnuniq, Jpg, Kumarsameer, Kuru, Ldimaggi, M4gnum0n, MC10, MER-C, Marasmusine, Mark Kilby, Marudubshinki, Matthewedwards, Michael Bernstein, Morrillonline, MrOllie, Nima.shahhosini, Nimowy, Notinasnaid, Octoferret, Ohnoitsjamie, OracleDBGuru, Pfhjvb0, ProfessionalTST, Qatutor, Qlabs impetus, Qtpautomation, Qwyrxian, R'n'B, RHaworth, Radagast83, Radiant!, Radiostationary, Raghublr, Rich Farmbrough, RichardHoultz, Rickjpelleg, Rjwilmsi, Robertvan1, Robinson Weijman, Ryadav, Ryepie, SSmithNY, Sbono, Shijuraj, Shlomif, Softwaretest1, Srideep TestPlant, Ssingaraju, SteveLoughran, Sundaramkumar, Swtechwr, Testautomator, Thv, Ttrevers, Tumaka, Tushar291081, Vadimka, Veledan, Versageek, Walter Görlitz, Webbbbbbber, Winmacro, Wrp103, Yan Kuligin, ZachGT, Zorgon7, 249 anonymous edits

iMacros *Source*: http://en.wikipedia.org/w/index.php?oldid=398852338 *Contributors*: Agentq314, AliveFreeHappy, Andreas Kaufmann, CharlesMGoodwin, CliffC, Digita, Dropmakeslucky, FastLizard4, FleetCommand, Ggaaron, JLaTondre, JamesMBrian, KenFehling, Luckydrink1, Mandarax, MarcDorso, Megaadmin8, Newtown11, Oneforfortytwo, PGPirate, Pinecar, Pinkano, R'n'B, Starofale, Timo53, Timstanford, Underpants, Webbyawards, 59 anonymous edits

Abnormal end *Source*: http://en.wikipedia.org/w/index.php?oldid=393269145 *Contributors*: Adamdaley, Bingobangobongoboo, Bobblewik, Cea801, Censorship Workaround, Damian Yerrick, Damuna, Dfletter, Droob, Ellmist, Emperorbma, Erkan Yilmaz, Fenice, Joeblakesley, JonHarder, Loadmaster, Mirror Vax, RTC, Rich Farmbrough, Rwwww, Sgeureka, Shinmawa, SimonP, Teehee123, 11 anonymous edits

Anomaly in software *Source*: http://en.wikipedia.org/w/index.php?oldid=345456507 *Contributors*: Ais523, Anthony Appleyard, Bryan Derksen, Damadm00, Dawkeye, Erkan Yilmaz, Furrykef, Gavia immer, Javaguy223, Jkl, Maliz, Ouzo, Romanski, Undeference, Wenli, Woohookitty, 5 anonymous edits

C Traps and Pitfalls *Source*: http://en.wikipedia.org/w/index.php?oldid=386704629 *Contributors*: BenFrantzDale, DESiegel, Dancter, Erkan Yilmaz, Goat-see, Halo, MakeRocketGoNow, Marudubshinki, Maustrauser, Mmernex, Mrwojo, PGSONIC, Pegship, Piet Delport, Reyk, Ruud Koot, Suruena, Tony Sidaway, Vinodxx1, Wernher, Wikiklrsc, 6 anonymous edits

Crash (computing) *Source*: http://en.wikipedia.org/w/index.php?oldid=392634673 *Contributors*: 1a2c, Alvarokr, Andycjp, Armiris, Arvindn, B.duck, Barefootguru, BenRG, Bluefoxicy, Cactus26, Catgut, Ccox@adobe.com, CryptoDerk, Curps, Cwenger, CyberSkull, Daemorris, Danakil, DataMatrix, Derek Ross, Deville, Dotman557, Dwedit, Dysprosia, Edward, Erkan Yilmaz, Freakofnurture, Fuzzyslob, GRAHAMUK, Guinness2702, Harryboyles, Hermione99, Home Row Keysplurge, I do not exist, Jake Nelson, JonHarder, Joy, Jpbowen, Kbdank71, Kozuch, Ligulem, Linguofreak, M4gnum0n, MattGiuca, Miguel Andrade, Mipadi, Mr.Z-man, Msikma, Mtu, Nabla, Nasa-verve, Neale Monks, Night Gyr, Nopira, Nwwaew, Pcu123456789, Philip Howard, Pinecar, Piroroadkill, Plague006, Querswpoia, R. S. Shaw, Roadmr, Rsduhamel, RzR, ST47, SchuminWeb, Sex was great, Shawnc, Sonic3, Splintax, Sum0, TechPurism, UberScienceNerd, Uncle G, WhiteCrane, Wiknerd, Wile E. Heresiarch, Wilsonsamm, Woohookitty, Yamla, 82 anonymous edits

Crash to desktop *Source*: http://en.wikipedia.org/w/index.php?oldid=393810501 *Contributors*: AverageGuy, Bryan Seecrets, CesarB, Chatfecter, Coolbho3000, DemonThing, Erkan Yilmaz, Funandtrvl, Furrykef, Greenrd, IIVQ, JaradT, JonHarder, JuWiki2, Kathleen.wright5, MattGiuca, ModusOperandi, Mscudder, Pcarbonn, Robofish, Starkiller88, SuperHamster, Teehee123, Tommy Kronkvist, Vendettax, 13 anonymous edits

Deadlock *Source*: http://en.wikipedia.org/w/index.php?oldid=399946451 *Contributors*: ...adam..., 5 albert square, Adam78, Adib.roumani, Alansohn, Aldie, AlexFili, Alexie, AlistairMcMillan, Allan McInnes, Antandrus, Aragorn2, Archelon, Auntof6, Begoon, Betacommand, Biker Biker, Caltas, Caper13, Capricorn42, Ccacsmss, Chaos.squirrel, Charles Matthews, Chodorkovskiy, Clausen, CobaltBlue, Coffeehood, Comps, Corti, Cybercobra, DMCer, Darshana.jayasinghe, Dereckson, Derek Ross, Discospinster, Dmr2, Dori, Dysprosia, E Wing, Earthlyreason, Elkman, Eloquence, Erik Sandberg, Erkan Yilmaz, Fikril, Frecklefoot, Fredrik, Fresheneesz, Fyyer, George Leung, Glass Sword, Greensburger, Hashproduct, Helder Ribeiro, Hkmaly, Hpitkala, Hu12, Hv, JCLately, JRaber, JSpung, Jbalint, Jeffhos, Jncraton, Jnlin, JonHarder, Jusdafax, Kaustav 28061987, Kbdank71, Kenyon, Kunalthakar, Kzollman, LapoLuchini, Larry V, Larsk1985, Legis, LilHelpa, LjL, Lobner, M4gnum0n, MBelgrano, MBisanz, MagiMaster, Manav 95, Mandarax, Martarius, Matiwiki, MatthewWilcox, Maury Markowitz, Maxim Razin, McGeddon, Michael Hardy, Mikeo, Miym, Mpa, Mrholybrain, Neilc, NerdyScienceDude, Normxxx, Ohanian, Opelio, Orphan Wiki, OverlordQ, Parsiferon, Pepper, Peter Horn, Piano non troppo, Piet Delport, Pravin S. Pandey, Prodego, Psyche, Qfennessy, Quiark, R'n'B, RA0808, RJFJR, Radagast83, Rajashar, Randomalious, Rdenis, Reconsider the static, Reedy, Samw, Sander, Sanders muc, Scooter, Seb az86556, Sergio PJ, SigmaEpsilon, SimonP, Skorgu, Slamb, So Awesome, Sonicsuns, Sst557, Stephenb, Sth.pratik, Stickee, Svick, THEN WHO WAS PHONE?, TamusJRoyce, Tan20011, Tavilis, Tewk, The Anome, The Nut, Thegeneralguy, Thomas Larsen, Trusilver, Urhixidur, VictorAnyakin, Vocaro, Vonsche, Web-Crawling Stickler, Webvamsi555, WhosAsking, Wik, Wikiklrsc, WikipedianMarlith, Xvr, Yvwv, Zero sharp, Zvar, 360 anonymous edits

Debugger *Source*: http://en.wikipedia.org/w/index.php?oldid=399682533 *Contributors*: 16@r, A. B., A5b, AS, Abdull, Acagney, Adriatikus, Aivosto, Alastaird, Ancheta Wis, AnhadSingh, Auric, Bheron, Bryan Derksen, Caputt, Carmencr, Charivari, Checkshirt, ChrisRuvolo, Collect, Conti, Convex hull, Czambra, D-Rock, Dav4is, Delirium, Dodji.seketeli, Drmies, Econrad, Erkan Yilmaz, FF2010, Fauxpoefoes, FilippoGioachin, George Schmidt, GerardM, Ghettoblaster, Giftlite, Hasenstr, Hgfernan, Hongguo, Ike-bana, InTheCastle, JPats, Jehnavi, Jmath666, JonathonReinhart, Jorgon, Jéské Couriano, Jóna Þórunn, Kbdank71, Kdakin, Kekedada, Kelvinclayne, Khalid hassani, Leonard G., Lo2u, Lzur, Markusaachen, Marudubshinki, MattGiuca, Mike Van Emmerik, Mikeblas, Mipadi, Mircea.Vutcovici, Mirror Vax, Moa3333, Mshonle, Naterice, Navalg, Nlfiedler, Oli Filth, Pinecar, Psychonaut, Ptrb, Quuxplusone, RabbleRouser, Raevel, ReneS, Robert Merkel, Rodrigob, Rootbeer, Sabine Kreidl, Sandrarossi, Schultkl, SchuminWeb, Schzmo, ScottDavis, SexHex, Shane Lawrence, Simetrical, SimonP, SkyWalker, Snigbrook, Speedplane, Square87, Stan Shebs, Stassats, Stephen Gilbert, Swtechwr, THF, Tigrisek, Tqbf, TraumaPony, Txomin, Unforgettableid, Unomi, Uzume, Warren, Wernher, Wgdominic, Witchinghour, X., YUL89YYZ, Yonkie, Yworo, ZacBowling, 113 anonymous edits

Division by zero *Source*: http://en.wikipedia.org/w/index.php?oldid=399728462 *Contributors*: 1diot, 21655, Abdull, Adam1213, AeonicOmega, Aetheling, Afuller2028, Akira625, Alansohn, Aleph4, AlexChurchill, AlexiusHoratius, Alison, Allstarecho, Am Fiosaigear, Amatulic, Ams80, AngelOfSadness, Animum, Anonymous Dissident, Antandrus, Artaxiad, Ash-ds, Asmeurer, Astronouth7303, Atif.t2, Atropos, AuburnPilot, AugPi, Autonova, AxelBoldt, AzaToth, BD2412, Badgernet, BenFrantzDale, Berserkerz Crit, Black Carrot, Bobo192, Bowlhover, Brendan Moody, Brighterorange, Brokenverse, Bubmaster337, BunnyBuns, CBM, CRGreathouse, CSTAR, Cadillac, Calexico, Camiloatua, Can't sleep, clown will eat me, CanisRufus, Capricorn42, Captain Cheeks, Charles Matthews, CheeseSucker, Chemicalinterest, Chessphoon, Church of emacs, Clarince63, CompuHacker, Comrade42, Conan-san, Cortezz, Courcelles, Crapper123456, Cremepuff222, Cybercobra, DVdm, Daleh, Dalstadt, Damian Yerrick, Daniel Case, Daniel15, Danlev, Darth Panda, David Eppstein, DeadEyeArrow, Death motor, Deeptrivia, Deirdre, Delirium, Denelson83, Deville, DiscordantNote, Discospinster, Divideby0, Dmcq, Doctormatt, Dogah, Domestic Correction, Dominic, DragonflySixtyseven, Dragoran, Dream out loud, Dreddlox, Drunkenmonkey, Dugwiki, DwS, ESkog, Ebeisher, Eep², Efansay, Ehrenkater, Epbr123, Erkan Yilmaz, Ernest lk lam, Eronixpress, Ethlogen, Evil saltine, EvilBrak, Feinoha, FilipeS, FirmBenevolence, Flewis, Flip619, Frecklefoot, Fredrik, Freenaulij, Furfagswin, Furrykef, Fyyer, G, Gaiacarra, Gail, Gandalf61, Gaël J., George2001hi, Giftlite, Gil Dawson, Glacier Wolf, Goodnightmush, Graue, Guanaco, Gurch, H, Halanon, Hanacy, HappyInGeneral, Heimstern, Hellbus, Henrygb, HereToHelp, Honza Záruba, Hyperdeath, Hypers36, IGeMiNix, Ianmathwiz7,

Incrediblub, Interested2, Into The Fray, Ironiridis, It Is Me Here, J.delanoy, JForget, JNW, JRSpriggs, Ja 62, JaGa, Jao, Jeff G., Jeremy Visser, Jesper Carlstrom, Jesse Viviano, Jitse Niesen, Jonathan de Boyne Pollard, Josh Parris, Jpatokal, JuWiki2, JuneGloom07, Katzmik, Kaysakado, Kelly Denham, Kenyon, KevinRachel2010, Kevinoesef, Kieff, Kprateek88, Krsont, Ktims, Kubigula, Kurisu, Kwithak, LDCutter, LOLIHASACCOUNT, La goutte de pluie, Landon1980, Larsvolta, Lavenderbunny, Lethe, Liastnir, Liftarn, Lildoodle, Linas, Lkjhgfdsa, Loadmaster, Logical2u, Lukeelms, Luminon, Luna Santin, MC10, Maclean25, Madhero88, Magioladitis, Majopius, Malo, MasamuneXGP, MattGiuca, Mattbrundage, Mattrn96, Matwilko, Mawfive, McGeddon, Mcozy09, Mdntth, Mel Etitis, Melchoir, Meme133ere, Meni Rosenfeld, Metacomet, Mets501, Mgiganteus1, MiNombreDeGuerra, Michael Hardy, MightyWarrior, Mild Bill Hiccup, MilitaryTarget, Mindmatrix, Misantropo, Mobile1551, Mobius131186, Mrjeff, Mshonle, Muro de Aguas, Mwtoews, NOrbeck, NYKevin, Najoj, Nate1481, NellieBly, Netalarm, Nikkimaria, Ninetyone, Ninly, Nokternus420, NuclearWarfare, Octahedron80, Oleg Alexandrov, OllieFury, OrangeAipom, Out-of-focus, PMLawrence, PV=nRT, Papre, Patrick, Paul August, Paul from Michigan, PaulKanter, Pepper, Petershen1984, Pfalstad, Phantomsteve, Pharaoh of the Wizards, Piano non troppo, Pigsonthewing, Pinethicket, Plasticup, Plastikspork, Polly, Pomte, Prodego, Psb777, Pseudomonas, QRX, Quuxplusone, RDBury, Reach Out to the Truth, Repku, Revolver, Reywas92, Rich Farmbrough, Rick Norwood, Roadrunner, Robo37, Ron2, Rpvdk, Rsrikanth05, Ruud Koot, SJP, ST47, Salix alba, Samofshs11, Sanfranman59, SchfiftyThree, Scott Gall, Scott5114, Sct72, Sdasdadattt, Shadow1, ShakingSpirit, Shawn81, ShunterAlhena, Silly rabbit, SirParagon, Sjö, Skunkboy74, Skäpperöd, Sligocki, Smappy, Smartie01, Smultiplication, Sockpuppetaccountlol, Somebody500, Sonjaaa, Sopoforic, Spinningspark, Spliffy, Spoofergirl, Squidoflint, StaticGull, StevenHidy, Stextc, StradivariusTV, Suffusion of Yellow, Syazwan1995, THEN WHO WAS PHONE?, THF, TaintedMustard, TakuyaMurata, Tempodivalse, Terryzturner, Thaurisil, The Thing That Should Not Be, The Utahraptor, TheCilver, TheKMan, Thestalosj, ThirdParty, Tide rolls, Tiles, Tkuvho, Tobias Bergemann, Toomai Glittershine, Touch Of Light, Trakesht, Trovatore, Tylerni7, Ultimus, Ungvichian, Username12321, Utcursch, Venu62, Versus22, Vistro, Vrenator, Wabitag, Walkerbristol, Way12go, Wdflake, WendelScardua, Wik, Wikiborg, Wikiboy12, Wikieditor06, Wile E. Heresiarch, Willking1979, Wimt, Winchelsea, Wkcp, Wolfrock, Wvbailey, Wwwwolf, Xonoro, Yamakiri, YeAaMsLtA, Zack, Zarel, ZeroOne, 608 anonymous edits

Easter egg (media) *Source*: http://en.wikipedia.org/w/index.php?oldid=399541615 *Contributors*: -Midorihana-, 1990bacon, A legend, ASarnat, Aaa111, Aaron Kauppi, Absolutely Curtains, Action Jackson IV, Adashiel, Addict 2006, Afn, Agapetos angel, Agatekartik, Alphabeter, Altenmann, Alvis, Amber388, Ancatdubh43, Andy, Anonymous Cow, Anthony Ivanoff, Anything Else, Apparition11, Armistej, Ashley Pomeroy, Ask123, Badger Drink, Baffle gab1978, Bart133, Basilwhite, BazookaJoe, Bevo, Bewildebeast, Bfinn, Binary2, Binduka, BioYu-Gi!, Biruitorul, BlaiseFEgan, Bletch, Bob f it, Bobbaxter, Bobet, Bradfregger, Brandon5485, Breynre, Brian Kendig, Brian Patrie, BrianRecchia, Briankervin, Bsrboy, Buddy13, CaliforniaAliBaba, Calmypal, CanisRufus, Capricorn42, Chappy84, Charles Nguyen, Chaser, Chicken people, Chris Chittleborough, ChrisCork, Clairewatson675, Codelad, Col. Sweeto, Computer97, Corti, Cprompt, Curps, Cwolfsheep, Céréales Killer, D4S, DARTH SIDIOUS 2, DJMcNiff, Daibhid C, Darcrist, Dark Shikari, Dark0805, Darkhorse, Dave.Dunford, David Latapie, Davidbspalding, Davidwil, Dawnseeker2000, DeadlyActs2k6, Debresser, DerHexer, Dfee, Discospinster, Djegan, Dlrohrer2003, Doktor Wilhelm, Drake Clawfang, Dreftymac, DropDeadGorgias, Dylanfromthenorth, Eclectic hippie, Ed Fitzgerald, Edlin2, Eekerz, Einstein runner, Epbr123, Erianna, Erkan Yilmaz, Eugenespeed, Evan1109, Evice, Falcon8765, Ferron321, Fethers, Fiftytwo thirty, Firien, Firsfron, FlocciNonFacio, Fragglet, Frecklefoot, Furrykef, GCord52, GVOLTT, Gaeamil, Gaius Cornelius, Geeked, Geneffects, Geoffrey, George Steinmetz, Gerbrant, Getcrunk, GeveraBert, Goatasaur, Golbez, Goldenband, Graham87, Gtrmp, Gunrun, Gurch, Gwernol, Haemo, Hamster2.0, Hanif248, Hapenny, Harepusen, Havarhen, Hede2000, Hellmark, Hirokazu, Hrab0001, Hu12, Hulmem, Hyad, IMSoP, IMattUK, Ian Fieggen, Ianholst, Ickle, Im.a.lumberjack, ImperviusXR, Iridescent, JHunterJ, JIP, JVRosenman, James086, Jasenlee, Jason Recliner, Esq., Jasonglchu, Javidjamae, Jay Firestorm, Jedimaster1000, Jeff Silvers, Jesse0986, Jesster79, Jezthepie, Jitka, Joanberenguer, Joe The Dragon, Joeblakesley, Joelholdsworth, John Darrow, John Stattic, Jor, Julyo, Juniglove, JustPhil, Katalaveno, Kathar, Kbdank71, KeKe, KieferSkunk, Kieff, Kimiko, Kjlewis, Klausmetzger, Kocio, Krashlandon, Kross, Kyng, LOL, Law, Le Messor, Lew Zealand IV, Lilac Soul, Lkjhgfdsa, LouScheffer, Luís Felipe Braga, MIT Trekkie, MaGioZal, Macintosh User, Mackeriv, Makron1n, Malick78, Malpass93, Marasmusine, Margin1522, Martyn Smith, Master gopher, Master of Puppets, Matty-chan, Matveims, Maximaximax, McB, McSly, Mdanh2002, Meaty Weenies, MegX, Mercury McKinnon, Metalion SOS, Michael Hardy, MichaelMatirko, Mighty Racoon, Mike 7, Mindeye, Miq, Mn1, Monkeynoze, Morenooso, Moreschi, MosheZadka, Mrmiscellanious, Ms2ger, Mskonline, Mvramesh99, Nealmcb, Neo12345292, Nick R, Nil Einne, Nintendax, Nixeagle, OGoncho, Ohnoitsjamie, Ohthelameness, Oink1234, Ol32, OliviaGuest, Ooglyboo, Orion2004, Ossipewsk, Pames jark, Peeknpoke, Peng, Petorial, Petri Krohn, Pgan002, Pikawil, Pink2wink, Popexvi, Ppareit, Prodego, Pumpkingrrl, Pwright329, QwerpQwertus, Radagast, Rae Logan, RaggieSoft, Rancor125, Rapido, Red Alien, RedWolf, Renesisevo, Rettetast, RexNL, Rfc1394, Rhindle The Red, Riana, Rjwilmsi, Robert Skyhawk, Roke, RoyBatty42, Ryan shell, RyanCross, RyanDesign, Salamurai, Sars, SaucyWench, Sc0ur, ScaldingHotSoup, SchuminWeb, Sebras, Secret Saturdays, ShadowMan1od, Sheridan, Sicherlich, Sidasta, Sigmundur, SimonP, Sketchmoose, Skylights76, Slash's snakepit, SmartGuy, Sonic3KMaster, SonicBlue, Sordan, Soundcomm, Spellmaster, Staecker, StephenBuxton, Stephenchou0722, Stevenj, Sticky Light, Stratman, Svetovid, Sydius, Synetech, Szajd, Takuthehedgehog, Tantalos, Tempshill, The Rogue Penguin, The Ungovernable Force, The Wookieepedian, TheQuaker, TheTruthiness, Tide rolls, Tmopkisn, TomEatsCake, Tony Sidaway, Toytoy, TreasuryTag, Tregoweth, Tualha, UnHoly, Uncuddly, User6985, Verne Equinox, ViperSnake151, Vlad, Vssun, Warren, Watman, Wayne Hardman, Wernher, Wgungfu, Wiki alf, WildMIKE123, Woohookitty, Ww, Wxidea, Yamamoto Ichiro, ZS, Zakstu, Zayani, ZeChinaman, Zephalis, ZhaoHong, Zondor, Птате, Михајло Анђелковић, 491 anonymous edits

Exception handling *Source*: http://en.wikipedia.org/w/index.php?oldid=398397888 *Contributors*: Aaron Rotenberg, Abarnea 2000, Abdull, Ahy1, Andreas Kaufmann, Andrew Hampe, Aomarks, Ascánder, Astatine, Auntof6, Aurelien, B-rat, BMF81, BenFrantzDale, Betterusername, Blaxthos, Bmaisonnier, Brockert, Btx40, BurntSky, C17GMaster, CSProfBill, Cadr, Caiyu, Cander0000, Chealer, Chesterloke, Chu Jetcheng, Danrah, Dasch, David.Monniaux, David.kaplan, Decltype, Demitsu, Derek farn, Descubes, Doug Bell, DropDeadGorgias, Edcolins, Elektrik Shoos, Enric Naval, Eric B. and Rakim, Erkan Yilmaz, Esap, Etaoin, EvanED, EvanGrim, Everyking, Ewlloyd, FabianNiemann, Feb30th1712, Firsfron, Fubar Obfusco, Furrykef, Fuzzie, Gaal, Gary King, Green caterpillar, Greenrd, HaeB, Hairy Dude, Hans Bauer, Harriv, Hcheney, Homerjay, Hosterweis, Hu12, I take exception, J Casanova, JLaTondre, Jeanfoucault, JimD, Jkl, John Vandenberg, Jonhanson, Joswig, Jóna Þórunn, Kavadi carrier, Kku, Kseg, Kulandai, LilHelpa, Linas, Lowellian, Lucio, Luís Felipe Braga, MONGO, Magnus Bakken, Mahadevan R, Marudubshinki, Massysett, Melah Hashamaim, Mike Fikes, Mikething, Mintleaf, Mipadi, Munificent, Musiphil, Naveen84nv, Nbarth, NeilFraser, Neilc, NickBush24, OranL, Orderud, Patrick, PdDemeter, Peterdjones, Phresnel, Pianohacker, Piet Delport, PrologFan, Prosfilaes, Ptrb, QuantumEngineer, Radagast83, Random832, RedWolf, Rjgodoy, Rling, Rufous, Runtime, SAE1962, ScottBlomquist, SeanProctor, Smeezekitty, Smyth, Sycomonkey, TheTito, Thecheesykid, Thecodemachine, Thomas Linder Puls, Tigrisek, TimBentley, Tmaufer, Tobias Bergemann, Tompsci, TotoBaggins, Triddle, TuukkaH, UtherSRG, Vald, Venugopal.ch, Veryfaststuff, Vicarious, Vocaro, Widefox, Xezbeth, Yerpo, Yoric, Ysangkok, Zark77, Zippanova, 204 anonymous edits

Fail soft *Source*: http://en.wikipedia.org/w/index.php?oldid=360152247 *Contributors*: Alvin Seville, CXCV, Dawynn, Dv82matt, Peanutbreath, RHaworth, Rpyle731, Sparklinn, 1 anonymous edits

Fault (technology) *Source*: http://en.wikipedia.org/w/index.php?oldid=332300217 *Contributors*: Beto, BirgitteSB, Brianvance14, Capricorn42, Erkan Yilmaz, Fradeve11, JonHarder, Kjkolb, Moe Epsilon, 3 anonymous edits

Fragile binary interface problem *Source*: http://en.wikipedia.org/w/index.php?oldid=386809288 *Contributors*: BenRG, Bluemoose, David Levy, Elysdir, Erkan Yilmaz, Furby100, JLaTondre, Jerryobject, Kbg, Ketiltrout, Kevinlipe, Kprateek88, Marudubshinki, Rich Farmbrough, Ruakh, Ruud Koot, Scope creep, The Anome, 9 anonymous edits

Glitch *Source*: http://en.wikipedia.org/w/index.php?oldid=399407765 *Contributors*: -Ozone-, 16@r, 21655, 2help, Agnorton, Ale jrb, Altenmann, Angtayan, Antaeus Feldspar, Arienh4, Army1987, AvayaLive, Bentmonkeycage, Blacksmith47, BlueAzure, BoltClock, Bongwarrior, Boxclocke, Brassdude, Buchraeumer, Bulbaboy, Catgut, ChiragPatnaik, Cloud20045, Cohenhoward12, Crystalespeon, Cue the Strings, Curtdbz, CyberSach, DMG413, DaL33T, DaProx, Dagerman, Dangerousnerd, DanielPharos, Darth Panda, Dattebayo321, Denis Barthel, Der Ausländer, DerHexer, Discospinster, Dkkicks, DopefishJustin, Download, Dudegirl99, East1999Gang, ElfQrin, Erkan Yilmaz, Esanchez7587, Everyking, FFD8, Feinoha, Final222, Fisel, Flarn2006, Fresheneesz, Furrykef, GT4GTR, GVOLTT, Gaius Cornelius, Gartist, Gastlyboy, Glenn, Glitchy123, Graham87, Gyroggearloose, Hadal, Heron, Hooperbloob, I like pants, Igordebraga, Ikanreed, Imroy, Ipi31415, Iridescence, JIP, JLaTondre, JRC3, Jak Inn Thee Been Stock, James Emtage, JamieS93, Jeroham, Jfruh, Julessaulnier, JustAGal, JzG, Kakurady, Kappa, Kbh3rd, Keenan Pepper, Kimchi.sg, Kingpin13, Kl4m, Klink258, Krótki, Kukini, Kylu, Latitude0116, Lawlore, Lenin and McCarthy, Lexor, Lhasapso, Liberatus, LilHelpa, Lindosland, Lindsayx, Longhair, Luk, Macbookair3140, Magister Mathematicae, Marasmusine, Marek69, Mario777Zelda, MarphyBlack, Maximus Rex, McGeddon, Megaman en m, Meggar, Merope, Michagal, Miller17CU94, Minimac, Mjf314, Monkeytrumpets, Mreza sadeghifar, Mrwojo, Mzxrules, Nandesuka, Natl1, Nbarth, Neko-chan, Nick Scratch, Northmeister99, NovaDog, OlEnglish, OldCollie, Omicronpersei8, Oscara, PeaceNT, Piano non troppo, Pinethicket, PsychoJosh, Qst, RCTV3, Rdsmith4, RememberMe, Retired username, Reyk, Rjwilmsi, RobBrisbane, RogueMomen, SLFLdr.Matt, SQUIDMACK, Sade, Screwupman, Seraphin, Sfrankel05, Shoepeddler, SilvaStorm, Sky Attacker, Slakr, Snori, SoniKirby, Stratadrake, Stylish Alastor the Stylish, Swedishmartin, Synvincent, Tabitha7685, Tanthalas39, Thatguyflint, TheMadBaron, Thibbs, Tide rolls, Timl2k4, Tiptoety, Tlotoxl, TreasuryTag, Tregoweth, Twang, Twistedkombat, Tymoguin, Ufim, UltimateNintendoFan, Ultimus, Unixguy, Unknownperson1234, Veracosa, Wereon, Wikidaily2, Wikieditor06, WoodenTaco, Woohookitty, Wtshymanski, Xenon54, Xlegionx, Xpac252, YeshuaDavid, ZS, Zerokitsune, Zondor, 331 anonymous edits

Glitch art *Source*: http://en.wikipedia.org/w/index.php?oldid=395670187 *Contributors*: 7, Clomen Nature, Discospinster, Freshacconci, Gartist, Grigorievna, Kencf0618, Marasmusine, Martarius, Nbarth, Otisjimmy1, Pointillist, Wolfsheep113, 32 anonymous edits

Glitching *Source*: http://en.wikipedia.org/w/index.php?oldid=396924616 *Contributors*: 1970doc666, Addict 2006, AlexanderTG, Balloonguy, Big Oto, Birdman234, Blakegripling ph, Chrisdb89, Commander Shepard, Crass Spektakel, Cruncher, Dangerzone50, Dawynn, Drgn22178, E Wing, East1999Gang, Ele9699, FeldBum, Ferloft101, Flarn2006, Hiddenfromview, Hooperbloob, JForget, Jeremyharmon, Jpgordon, Kappa, King of Hearts, Kung Fu Man, Lankiveil, Marasmusine, McGeddon, Michael A. White, Millionsandbillions, Mmldiz, Mogoyogo, Mydoctor93, Nicholas Weiner, Number13lucky, Pagrashtak, Pompadis, Reyk, Ric36, Rockittt, Rpyle731, Set84, Snigbrook, Spazure, Th3 Conduct0R, The Utahraptor, The last username left was taken, Thej42, TyrantX, Vendettax, WikiDaily, Wikidaily2, 83 anonymous edits

Handle leak *Source*: http://en.wikipedia.org/w/index.php?oldid=383411565 *Contributors*: Aivosto, ArtemRazin, Bruce1ee, Cmdrjameson, Elagatis, Erkan Yilmaz, GregorB, JH-man, JonHarder, Jvhertum, Longhair, Mrwojo, Neilm, Slordak, TheParanoidOne, Tobias Bergemann, 3 anonymous edits

Hang (computing) *Source*: http://en.wikipedia.org/w/index.php?oldid=398209670 *Contributors*: AGToth, Alkivar, Animeronin, Anthony Appleyard, Azikala, Buchanan-Hermit, Ccox@adobe.com, Cenarium, Cwenger, CyberSkull, DJ Clayworth, Danhash, Dave, Discospinster, Dylan Lake, EarthFurst, Elassint, Erkan Yilmaz, Evil saltine, Ewlyahoocom, Funandtrvl, Furrykef, Fuzzbox, G.hartig, Geniac, Gerry Ashton, Haakon, I do not exist, Jake Nelson, Jared Hunt, LonelyPker, Lowellian, Mailer diablo, Malfet, Mats131, Mike.Scheglov, Mr Gronk,

Muhandes, Nasa-verve, NawlinWiki, Patrick Maitland, Pedant17, Psyche, Rdsmith4, Shmo5, Sjwk, Starkiller88, Tabletop, Tatewbaker, TheJames, TimMagic, Tyler.szabo, Voyagerfan5761, Yurik, 44 anonymous edits

Heap overflow *Source*: http://en.wikipedia.org/w/index.php?oldid=393668099 *Contributors*: Abaddon314159, AlistairMcMillan, AnnaP, Chris the speller, Christan80, Dysprosia, Erik9, Erkan Yilmaz, Extinguisher, Fathisules, Franck Dernoncourt, Ghbarratt, HeiseUK, Improv, Jrincayc, Karada, Leeor net, Lssilva, Maduskis, Smaffy, StephenFalken, Tompsci, Trou, Wapcaplet, Zundark, 44 anonymous edits

Interrupt storm *Source*: http://en.wikipedia.org/w/index.php?oldid=363335519 *Contributors*: Abdull, Cmdrjameson, Exaton, Fuzzbox, Golbez, Ham Pastrami, Hooperbloob, Illythr, Jake Nelson, Jsmethers, Larytet, Mirror Vax, Mmom, Quuxplusone, Reisio, Storkk, The Anome, Trasz, Wayne Hardman, Willy Wonka on Wheels!, 12 anonymous edits

Memory leak *Source*: http://en.wikipedia.org/w/index.php?oldid=394195163 *Contributors*: .:Ajvol:., 16@r, 666666th user, Alfio, AliveFreeHappy, Ancheta Wis, Andrew Eng, Andrewsamuels1988, Android Mouse, Andytuba, Apelleti, Arof, Bartledan, Beland, Bryan Derksen, Capi, ChrisRuvolo, Christian *Yendi* Severin, Conversion script, Crislee 88, Cybersnoopy, DannyKitty, Darrien, Dgies, DominicCronin, Doug Bell, Dragon 280, Dysprosia, ESkog, Edcolins, ElKevbo, EncMstr, Erkan Yilmaz, EvilGuru, FancyMouse, FlyingParrot, Frigoris, Furrykef, GNU, Gareth Owen, Garo, Guido del Confuso, Gvcormac, Haham hanuka, Haish2, Hammer Raccoon, HenryLi, Hervegirod, Hooperbloob, Hydrargyrum, Incnis Mrsi, JeLuF, Jeffab123, JonHarder, Juan Ponderas, K.Nevelsteen, Kbolino, Kenny sh, Khono, Korath, Kwsn, LOL, Leenakhunte, Leibniz, Lightning, Llywrch, Lofote, Luís Felipe Braga, Lvlin, MK8, Matikkapoika, Mboverload, Milan Keršláger, Mind my edits, Mintleaf, Moriori, Nick Garvey, Nilfanion, Ninly, Notinasnaid, Ojolali Yo, Olathe, Oleg Alexandrov, Orderud, PamD, Pfortuny, Philip Trueman, Polonium, Razorflame, RedWolf, Rror, Rv74, Sandos, Shinuvk, Sikon, Snailwalker, Snaxe920, StuartBrady, Sundar2000, The Anome, TheListUpdater, Tomoyo, Tustin2121, Watcher, Wikante, Wrp103, Ww, Xpclient, 200 anonymous edits

NaN *Source*: http://en.wikipedia.org/w/index.php?oldid=398814149 *Contributors*: 0, Andjam, Anthony Appleyard, Anthonyjameswood, ArnoldReinhold, Arthur Rubin, Audriusa, AySz88, BadgerBadger, Bbi5291, Bobo192, Brianjd, Brighterorange, CRGreathouse, Cfeet77, Charles Matthews, Chowbok, CiaPan, Classicalecon, Coffee2theorems, Copyeditor42, Cyp, Dcoetzee, Dmcq, Dmn, Dpv, Duncan, Epbr123, Erkan Yilmaz, Eternalschala, Farosdaughter, Fresheneesz, Gah4, Gary King, Glrx, Graemec2, Graue, H, HappyDog, Hkhk59333, J.delanoy, Jackaranga, JakeVortex, Jh51681, Jkt, Jmah, Jshadias, Katieh5584, Kbdank71, Keith111, Keka, Kidx, Kloff, LOL, Macrakis, Maurreen, Melchoir, Merope, Mfc, Michael Hardy, Mike Rosoft, Mikewill, Muro de Aguas, NickyMcLean, Obscurans, OverlordQ, PGSONIC, PTC enterprises, Paul from Michigan, Petter Strandmark, Pseudomonas, Puckly, Random832, Rwwww, Saccerzd, Salix alba, Sam Hocevar, Sduden, Shanel, Showtime2009, Shyamal, Soccerhead123456789, Stevenj, Subversive.sound, Svick, TakuyaMurata, Thetorpedodog, Thorenn, Tobias Bergemann, Tom Duff, Ultimus, Uncle G, Vald, Valodzka, Vincent Lefèvre, Warren, Wikipedian06, Woody, 92 anonymous edits

Negative cache *Source*: http://en.wikipedia.org/w/index.php?oldid=332348476 *Contributors*: Alnokta, Dylan anglada, El C, Eloquence, Erkan Yilmaz, Fubar Obfusco, Ganymead, Gracefool, Hooperbloob, Intgr, JesseW, Kubanczyk, Malo, Marudubshinki, Nimur, Paddu, Piet Delport, Pxma, TakuyaMurata, Thumperward, Wapcaplet, 7 anonymous edits

Software aging *Source*: http://en.wikipedia.org/w/index.php?oldid=327576115 *Contributors*: Accessory, Andreas Kaufmann, Fabrictramp, Malcolma, Rmatiasjr, Tobias Bergemann, 2 anonymous edits

Stack buffer overflow *Source*: http://en.wikipedia.org/w/index.php?oldid=398034501 *Contributors*: Abaddon314159, Akira625, Alcapwned86, Askari Mark, C. A. Russell, Dougofborg, Erik9, Fathisules, Fooblizoo, Irishguy, Lukedrummond, Macbutch, Mathiasl26, Michael B. Trausch, NeonMerlin, Nibios, Oli Filth, Otto42, Pastore Italy, Pdelong, Pengo, PrestonH, Qwerty0, Rdancer, RedWolf, RegRCN, Rjwilmsi, Rossenglish, Samadam, Simetrical, Skyy Train, StephenFalken, Teimu.tm, Teraman, The Anome, Tompsci, Xmm0, Zecured, 49 anonymous edits

Stale pointer bug *Source*: http://en.wikipedia.org/w/index.php?oldid=306358103 *Contributors*: Elf, Emeraude, Erkan Yilmaz, Heron, Hooperbloob, Mrwojo, Nneonneo, Ospalh, Somercet, Stewartadcock, Tardis, Template namespace initialisation script, Zoicon5, 4 anonymous edits

Image Sources, Licenses and Contributors

Image:USB_flash_drive.JPG *Source*: http://en.wikipedia.org/w/index.php?title=File:USB_flash_drive.JPG *License*: GNU Free Documentation License *Contributors*: User:Nrbelex

Image:Dg-nova3.jpg *Source*: http://en.wikipedia.org/w/index.php?title=File:Dg-nova3.jpg *License*: unknown *Contributors*: User Qu1j0t3 on en.wikipedia

Image:Imacros.png *Source*: http://en.wikipedia.org/w/index.php?title=File:Imacros.png *License*: unknown *Contributors*: FleetCommand, Sqawizard

Image:Blue Screen Phone.jpg *Source*: http://en.wikipedia.org/w/index.php?title=File:Blue_Screen_Phone.jpg *License*: Public Domain *Contributors*: Editor at Large, Edward, J o, Mormegil, Pbm, Railwayfan2005, Tommy Kronkvist, Wesha, 2 anonymous edits

Image:Computer crash airport.jpg *Source*: http://en.wikipedia.org/w/index.php?title=File:Computer_crash_airport.jpg *License*: Public Domain *Contributors*: Miguel Andrade, 1 anonymous edits

Image:Winpdb-1.3.6.png *Source*: http://en.wikipedia.org/w/index.php?title=File:Winpdb-1.3.6.png *License*: GNU General Public License *Contributors*: Winpdb is released under GPLv2 (or any later version). Copyright (C) 2005-2008 Nir Aides.

File:Hyperbola one over x.svg *Source*: http://en.wikipedia.org/w/index.php?title=File:Hyperbola_one_over_x.svg *License*: Creative Commons Attribution-Sharealike 2.5 *Contributors*: Anarkman, Darapti, Juiced lemon, Ktims, Myself488, 6 anonymous edits

File:SpeedCrunch divide by zero.png *Source*: http://en.wikipedia.org/w/index.php?title=File:SpeedCrunch_divide_by_zero.png *License*: GNU General Public License *Contributors*: Simeon Higgs

File:TI86_Calculator_DivByZero.jpg *Source*: http://en.wikipedia.org/w/index.php?title=File:TI86_Calculator_DivByZero.jpg *License*: Public Domain *Contributors*: User:Torindkflt

File:Stickies v.1.0.4 Easter Egg.png *Source*: http://en.wikipedia.org/w/index.php?title=File:Stickies_v.1.0.4_Easter_Egg.png *License*: unknown *Contributors*: MaGioZal

Image:Codglitch3.jpg *Source*: http://en.wikipedia.org/w/index.php?title=File:Codglitch3.jpg *License*: Public Domain *Contributors*: WikiDaily

File:Sample sawtooth.jpg *Source*: http://en.wikipedia.org/w/index.php?title=File:Sample_sawtooth.jpg *License*: Public Domain *Contributors*: User:Jeffab123

Image:Stack Overflow 2.png *Source*: http://en.wikipedia.org/w/index.php?title=File:Stack_Overflow_2.png *License*: Public Domain *Contributors*: User:Abaddon314159

Image:Stack Overflow 3.png *Source*: http://en.wikipedia.org/w/index.php?title=File:Stack_Overflow_3.png *License*: Public Domain *Contributors*: User:Abaddon314159

Image:Stack Overflow 4.png *Source*: http://en.wikipedia.org/w/index.php?title=File:Stack_Overflow_4.png *License*: Public Domain *Contributors*: User:Abaddon314159

License

NU Free Documentation License Version 1.2, ovember 2002 Copyright (C) 2000,2001,2002 ree Software Foundation, Inc. 59 Temple lace, Suite 330, Boston, MA 02111 -1307 USA veryone is permitted to copy and distribute erbatim copies of this license documen t, but hanging it is not allowed.

PREAMBLE

'he purpose of this License is to make a manual, textbook, or ther functional and useful document "free" in the sense of eedom: to assure everyone the effective freedom to copy and distribute it, with or without modifying it, either commercially or oncommercially. Secondarily, this License preserves for the uthor and publisher a way to get credit for their work, while not eing considered responsible for modifications made by others. his License is a kind of "copyleft", which means that derivative orks of the document must themselves be free in the same ense. It complements the GNU General Public License, which is copyleft license designed for free software. We have designed is License in order to use it for manuals for free software, ecause free software needs free documentation: a free program hould come with manuals providing the same freedoms that the oftware does. But this License is not limited to software manuals; can be used for any textual work, regardless of subject matter whether it is published as a printed book. We recommend this icense principally for works whose purpose is instruction or eference.

APPLICABILITY AND DEFINITIONS

'his License applies to any manual or ot her work, in any edium, that contains a notice placed by the copyright holder aying it can be distributed under the terms of this License. Such notice grants a world -wide, royalty -free license, unlimited in uration, to use that work under the conditio ns stated herein. The Document", below, refers to any such manual or work. Any ember of the public is a licensee, and is addressed as "you". ou accept the license if you copy, modify or distribute the work a way requiring permission under copyright l aw. A "Modified ersion" of the Document means any work containing the ocument or a portion of it, either copied verbatim, or with odifications and/or translated into another language. A Secondary Section" is a named appendix or a front -matter ection o f the Document that deals exclusively with the lationship of the publishers or authors of the Document to the ocument's overall subject (or to related matters) and contains othing that could fall directly within that overall subject. (Thus, if e Document is in part a textbook of mathematics, a Secondary ection may not explain any mathematics.) The relationship could e a matter of historical connection with the subject or with elated matters, or of legal, commercial, philosophical, ethical or olitical position regarding them. The "Invariant Sections" are ertain Secondary Sections whose titles are designated, as being ose of Invariant Sections, in the notice that says that the ocument is released under this License. If a section does not fit e above definition of Secondary then it is not allowed to be esignated as Invariant. The Document may contain zero ivariant Sections. If the Document does not identify any Invariant ections then there are none. The "Cover Texts" are certain short assages of text that are listed, as Front -Cover Texts or Back - over Texts, in the notice that says that the Document is eleased under this License. A Front -Cover Text may be at most words, and a Back -Cover Text may be at most 25 words. A Transparent" copy of the Document means a machine -readable opy, represented in a format whose specification is available to e general public, that is suitable for revising the document traightforwardly with generic text editors or (for images omposed of pixels) generic p aint programs or (for drawings) ome widely available drawing editor, and that is suitable for input o text formatters or for automatic translation to a variety of ormats suitable for input to text formatters. A copy made in an therwise Transparent file format whose markup, or absence of arkup, has been arranged to thwart or discourage subsequent odification by readers is not Transparent. An image format is ot Transparent if used for any substantial amount of text. A copy at is not "Transparent" is called "Opaque". Examples of suitable ormats for Transparent copies include plain ASCII without arkup, Texinfo input format, LaTeX input format, SGML or XML sing a publicly available DTD, and standard -conforming simple HTML, PostScript or PDF designed f or human modification. Examples of transparent image formats include PNG, XCF and PG. Opaque formats include proprietary formats that can be ead and edited only by proprietary word processors, SGML or (ML for which the DTD and/or processing tools are not generally vailable, and the machine -generated HTML, PostScript or PDF roduced by some word processors for output purposes only. The Title Page" means, for a printed book, the title page itself, plus uch following pages as are needed to hold, legibly, the material his License requires to appear in the title page. For works in ormats which do not have any title page as such, "Title Page" neans the text near the most prominent appearance of the work's tle, preceding the beginning of the body of the te xt. A section Entitled XYZ" means a named subunit of the Document whose tle either is precisely XYZ or contains XYZ in parentheses ollowing text that translates XYZ in another language. (Here XYZ tands for a specific section name mentioned below, such as Acknowledgements", "Dedications", "Endorsements", or History".) To "Preserve the Title" of such a section when you odify the Document means that it remains a section "Entitled (YZ" according to this definition. The Document may include Varranty Disc laimers next to the notice which states that this icense applies to the Document. These Warranty Disclaimers re considered to be included by reference in this License, but nly as regards disclaiming warranties: any other implication that hese Warranty Disclaimers may have is void and has no effect n the meaning of this License.

. VERBATIM COPYING

You may copy and distribute the Document in any medium, ither commercially or noncommercially, provided that this icense, the copyright notices, and the license notice saying this License applies to the Document are reproduced in all copies, and that you add no other conditions whatsoever to those of this License. You may not use technical measures to obstruct or control the reading or further copying of t he copies you make or distribute. However, you may accept compensation in exchange for copies. If you distribute a large enough number of copies you must also follow the conditions in section 3. You may also lend copies, under the same conditions stated ab ove, and you may publicly display copies.

3. COPYING IN QUANTITY

If you publish printed copies (or copies in media that commonly have printed covers) of the Document, numbering more than 100, and the Document's license notice requires Cover Texts, you must enclose the copies in covers that carry, clearly and legibly, all these Cover Texts: Front -Cover Texts on the front cover, and Back-Cover Texts on the back cover. Both covers must also clearly and legibly identify you as the publisher of these copies. The front cover must present the full title with all words of the title equally prominent and visible. You may add other material on the covers in addition. Copying with changes limited to the covers, as long as they preserve the title of the Document and s atisfy these conditions, can be treated as verbatim copying in other respects. If the required texts for either cover are too voluminous to fit legibly, you should put the first ones listed (as many as fit reasonably) on the actual cover, and continue the rest onto adjacent pages. If you publish or distribute Opaque copies of the Document numbering more than 100, you must either include a machine-readable Transparent copy along with each Opaque copy, or state in or with each Opaque copy a computer -network location from which the general network -using public has access to download using public -standard network protocols a complete Transparent copy of the Document, free of added material. If you use the latter option, you must take reasonably prudent steps, when you begin distribution of Opaque copies in quantity, to ensure that this Transparent copy will remain thus accessible at the stated location until at least one year after the last time you distribute an Opaque copy (directly or through your agents or retailers) of that edition to the public. It is requested, but not required, that you contact the authors of the Document well before redistributing any large number of copies, to give them a chance to provide you with an updated version of the Document.

4. MODIFICATIONS

You may copy and distribute a Modified Version of the Document under the conditions of sections 2 and 3 above, provided that you release the Modified Version under precisely this License, with the Modified Version filling the role of the Do cument, thus licensing distribution and modification of the Modified Version to whoever possesses a copy of it. In addition, you must do these things in the Modified Version: A. Use in the Title Page (and on the covers, if any) a title distinct from that o f the Document, and from those of previous versions (which should, if there were any, be listed in the History section of the Document). You may use the same title as a previous version if the original publisher of that version gives permission. B. List on the Title Page, as authors, one or more persons or entities responsible for authorship of the modifications in the Modified Version, together with at least five of the principal authors of the Document (all of its principal authors, if it has fewer than f ive), unless they release you from this requirement. C. State on the Title page the name of the publisher of the Modified Version, as the publisher. D. Preserve all the copyright notices of the Document. E. Add an appropriate copyright notice for your modi fications adjacent to the other copyright notices. F. Include, immediately after the copyright notices, a license notice giving the public permission to use the Modified Version under the terms of this License, in the form shown in the Addendum below. G. Preserve in that license notice the full lists of Invariant Sections and required Cover Texts given in the Document's license notice. H. Include an unaltered copy of this License. I. Preserve the section Entitled "History", Preserve its Title, and add to it an item stating at least the title, year, new authors, and publisher of the Modified Version as given on the Title Page. If there is no section Entitled "History" in the Document, create one stating the title, year, authors, and publisher of the Document as given on its Title Page, then add an item describing the Modified Version as stated in the previous sentence. J. Preserve the network location, if any, given in the Document for public access to a Transparent copy of the Document, and likewise the netwo rk locations given in the Document for previous versions it was based on. These may be placed in the "History" section. You may omit a network location for a work that was published at least four years before the Document itself, or if the original publish er of the version it refers to gives permission. K. For any section Entitled "Acknowledgements" or "Dedications", Preserve the Title of the section, and preserve in the section all the substance and tone of each of the contributor acknowledgements and/or d edications given therein. L. Preserve all the Invariant Sections of the Document, unaltered in their text and in their titles. Section numbers or the equivalent are not considered part of the section titles. M. Delete any section Entitled "Endorsements". S uch a section may not be included in the Modified Version. N. Do not retitle any existing section to be Entitled "Endorsements" or to conflict in title with any Invariant Section. O. Preserve any Warranty Disclaimers. If the Modified Version includes new f ront-matter sections or appendices that qualify as Secondary Sections and contain no material copied from the Document, you may at your option designate some or all of these sections as invariant. To do this, add their titles to the list of Invariant Secti ons in the Modified Version's license notice. These titles must be distinct from any other section titles. You may add a section Entitled "Endorsements", provided it contains nothing but endorsements of your Modified Version by various parties --for example , statements of peer review or that the text has been approved by an organization as the authoritative definition of a standard. You may add a passage of up to five words as a Front -Cover Text, and a passage of up to 25 words as a Back -Cover Text, to the end of the list of Cover Texts in the Modified Version. Only one passage of Front-Cover Text and one of Back-Cover Text may be added by (or through arrangements made by) any one entity. If the Document already includes a cover text for the same cover, previously added by you or by arrangement made by the same entity you are acting on behalf of, you may not add another; but you may replace the old one, on explicit permission from the previous publisher that added the old one. The author(s) and publisher(s) of the Document do not by this License give permission to use their names for publicity for or to assert or imply endorsement of any Modified Version.

5. COMBINING DOCUMENTS

You may combine the Document with other documents released under this License, under the terms defined in section 4 above for modified versions, provided that you include in the combination all of the Invariant Sections of all of the original documents, unmodified, and list them all as Invariant Sections of your combined work in its lic ense notice, and that you preserve all their Warranty Disclaimers. The combined work need only contain one copy of this License, and multiple identical Invariant Sections may be replaced with a single copy. If there are multiple Invariant Sections with the same name but different contents, make the title of each such section unique by adding at the end of it, in parentheses, the name of the original author or publisher of that section if known, or else a unique number. Make the same adjustment to the sectio n titles in the list of Invariant Sections in the license notice of the combined work. In the combination, you must combine any sections Entitled "History" in the various original documents, forming one section Entitled "History"; likewise combine any sect ions Entitled "Acknowledgements", and any sections Entitled "Dedications". You must delete all sections Entitled "Endorsements".

6. COLLECTIONS OF DOCUMENTS

You may make a collection consisting of the Document and other documents released under this Lice nse, and replace the individual copies of this License in the various documents with a single copy that is included in the collection, provided that you follow the rules of this License for verbatim copying of each of the documents in all other respects. Y ou may extract a single document from such a collection, and distribute it individually under this License, provided you insert a copy of this License into the extracted document, and follow this License in all other respects regarding verbatim copying of that document.

7. AGGREGATION WITH INDEPENDENT WORKS

A compilation of the Document or its derivatives with other separate and independent documents or works, in or on a volume of a storage or distribution medium, is called an "aggregate" if the copyright resulting from the compilation is not used to limit the legal rights of the compilation's users beyond what the individual works permit. When the Document is included in an aggregate, this License does not apply to the other works in the aggregate which are not themselves derivative works of the Document. If the Cover Text requirement of section 3 is applicable to these copies of the Document, then if the Document is less than one half of the entire aggregate, the Document's Cover Texts may be placed on covers that bracket the Document within the aggregate, or the electronic equivalent of covers if the Document is in electronic form. Otherwise they must appear on printed covers that bracket the whole aggregate.

8. TRANSLATION

Translation is considered a k ind of modification, so you may distribute translations of the Document under the terms of section 4. Replacing Invariant Sections with translations requires special permission from their copyright holders, but you may include translations of some or all I nvariant Sections in addition to the original versions of these Invariant Sections. You may include a translation of this License, and all the license notices in the Document, and any Warranty Disclaimers, provided that you also include the original Englis h version of this License and the original versions of those notices and disclaimers. In case of a disagreement between the translation and the original version of this License or a notice or disclaimer, the original version will prevail. If a section in t he Document is Entitled "Acknowledgements", "Dedications", or "History", the requirement (section 4) to Preserve its Title (section 1) will typically require changing the actual title.

9. TERMINATION

You may not copy, modify, sublicense, or distribute th e Document except as expressly provided for under this License. Any other attempt to copy, modify, sublicense or distribute the Document is void, and will automatically terminate your rights under this License. However, parties who have received copies, or rights, from you under this License will not have their licenses terminated so long as such parties remain in full compliance.

10. FUTURE REVISIONS OF THIS LICENSE

The Free Software Foundation may publish new, revised versions of the GNU Free Documentat ion License from time to time. Such new versions will be similar in spirit to the present version, but may differ in detail to address new problems or concerns. See http://www.gnu.org/copyleft/. Each version of the License is given a distinguishing version number. If the Document specifies that a particular numbered version of this License "or any later version" applies to it, you have the option of following the terms and conditions either of that specified version or of any later version that has been pub lished (not as a draft) by the Free Software Foundation. If the Document does not specify a version number of this License, you may choose any version ever published (not as a draft) by the Free Software Foundation. ADDENDUM: How to use this License for yo ur documents To use this License in a document you have written, include a copy of the License in the document and put the following copyright and license notices just after the title page: Copyright (c) YEAR YOUR NAME. Permission is granted to copy, distr ibute and/or modify this document under the terms of the GNU Free Documentation License, Version 1.2 or any later version published by the Free Software Foundation; with no Invariant Sections, no Front -Cover Texts, and no Back-Cover Texts. A copy of the li cense is included in the section entitled "GNU Free Documentation License". If you have Invariant Sections, Front -Cover Texts and Back -Cover Texts, replace the "with...Texts." line with this: with the Invariant Sections being LIST THEIR TITLES, with the Fr ont-Cover Texts being LIST, and with the Back -Cover Texts being LIST. If you have Invariant Sections without Cover Texts, or some other combination of the three, merge those two alternatives to suit the situation. If your document contains nontrivial examp les of program code, we recommend releasing these examples in parallel under your choice of free software license, such as the GNU General Public License, to permit their use in free software.

CPSIA information can be obtained at www.ICGtesting.com
Printed in the USA
LVOW041649060812

293149LV00005B/64/P